TRUE CHAMPIONS KNOW THAT
SUCCESS TAKES SURRENDER...

SERVING

CHAD BONHAM, GENERAL EDITOR

FELLOWSHIP OF
CHRISTIAN ATHLETES

THE HEART AND SOUL IN SPORTS

Regal

From Gospel Light
Ventura, California, U.S.A.

Published by Regal
From Gospel Light
Ventura, California, U.S.A.
www.regalbooks.com
Printed in the U.S.A.

Library of Congress Cataloging-in-Publication Data
Serving / Fellowship of Christian Athletes.
p. cm.
ISBN-13: 978-0-8307-4579-1 (trade paper)
1. Athletes—Religious life. 2. Service (Theology) I. Fellowship of
Christian Athletes.
BV4596.A8S47 2008
241'.4—dc22
2008011573

1 2 3 4 5 6 7 8 9 10 / 15 14 13 12 11 10 09 08

Rights for publishing this book outside the U.S.A. or in non-English
languages are administered by Gospel Light Worldwide, an international
not-for-profit ministry. For additional information, please visit www.glww.org,
email info@glww.org, or write to Gospel Light Worldwide,
1957 Eastman Avenue, Ventura, CA 93003, U.S.A.

CONTENTS

The Four Core

Dan Britton
Senior Vice President of Ministries, Fellowship of Christian Athletes

The NCAA Final Four tournament is an exciting sporting event. Even if you are not a person who likes basketball, it is awesome to watch March Madness as it narrows down 64 teams into 4 core teams. This makes me think about Fellowship of Christian Athlete's "Four Core"—not four core teams, but four core values.

Core values are simply the way you live and conduct yourself. They are your attitudes, beliefs and convictions. Values should be what you are, not what you want to become. The goal is to embody your values every step of the way.

Are your values just words, or do you actually live them out? Can others identify the values in your life without your telling them? Your values need to be a driving force that shapes the way you do life! Talk is cheap, but values are valuable.

When everything is stripped away, what is left? For FCA, it is integrity, serving, teamwork and excellence. These Four Core are so powerful to me that I have made them my own personal values. So, I have to ask you, what are your values? What guides you? Let me share with you FCA's Four Core, which are even better than the Final Four!

Integrity

To have integrity means that you are committed to Christlike wholeness, both privately and publicly. Basically, it means to live without gaps. Proverbs 11:3 says that integrity should guide you, but that a double life will destroy you. You need to be transparent, authentic, honest and trustworthy. You should be the same in all situations and not become someone different when the competition of the game begins. Integrity means to act the same when no one is looking. It is not about being perfect, but, as a coach or athlete, you need to be the real deal.

Serving

In John 13:12-15, Jesus gives us the perfect example of serving when He washes the disciples' feet. He then commands the disciples to go and do unto others what He has done to them. How many of your teammates' feet have you washed? Maybe not literally, but spiritually, do you have an attitude of serving just as if you were washing their feet in the locker room? You need to seek out the needs of others and be passionate about pursuing people who are needy. And, the last time I checked, everyone is needy.

Teamwork

Teamwork means to work together with others and express unity in Christ in all of your relationships. In Philippians 2:1-5, Paul encourages each of us to be one, united together in spirit and purpose. We all need to be on one team—not just the team we play on, but on God's Team! We need to equip, encourage and empower one another. Do you celebrate and hurt together as teammates? You need to be arm-in-arm with others, locking up together to accomplish God's work. There should be no Lone Rangers.

Excellence

To pursue excellence means to honor and glorify God in everything you do. In Colossians 3:23-24, Paul writes, "whatever you do, work at it with all your heart, as working for the Lord, not for men." The "whatever" part is hard, because it means that everything you do must be done for God, not others. You need to pursue excellence in practice, in games, in schoolwork and in lifting weights. God deserves your best, not your leftovers.

It is tip-off time for the game of life. How will you be known?

Whatever happens, conduct yourselves in a manner worthy of the gospel of Christ.
PHILIPPIANS 1:27, *NIV*

Lord Jesus, my prayer is to live and compete with integrity, serving, teamwork and excellence. It is a high standard, but I know that with Your power and strength, it can happen. I want all my relationships to be known for things that are of You. Search my heart and reveal to me my values. I lay at the foot of the cross the values that do not honor You, and I ask for Your forgiveness. The values that bring You glory, I lay them at the foot of the cross for Your anointing.

THE HEART OF SERVING

As we dive into the core value of serving, we must realize that God calls everyone to serve. There is no one that is excluded from this value. It is not just for those who have the gift of serving or for those for whom it comes naturally. When we choose to serve others, we discover that there is power in serving others—not natural power, but supernatural power. It is not about getting power, but about giving power.

Many people serve so that they can be served, but this is not the type of serving that pleases God. The ultimate purpose of serving is for God's glory. After we have served others, we should say, "God is good," not "I am good."

The purpose of serving is to lift the name of Jesus. Rick Warren says, "We serve God by serving others. The world defines greatness in terms of power, possessions, prestige and position. In our self-serving culture with its me-first mentality, acting like a servant is not a popular concept." When we serve, we represent to the world what Jesus looks like.

The heart of serving is to take every gift, skill, talent and ability that God has given us and use it to serve others. That type of serving will stir the passion in our hearts. Each day, we should start by asking ourselves, *Who can I serve today?* Perhaps Samuel Chadwick nailed it best when he wrote, "Spirit-filled souls are ablaze for God. They love with a love that glows. They serve with a faith that kindles. They serve with a devotion that consumes."

When done right, serving is about love, not duty. When it is done out of love, joy is the byproduct of serving, not regret or guilt. Serving should come freely and not feel forced. It is an opportunity, not an obligation. We serve without thinking that we are going to get something back, because serving is about others, not self.

In Philippians, Paul challenges us to do nothing out of selfish ambition. We need to consider others better than ourselves, because self-denial is the core of serving. So, the tough question we need to ask ourselves is, *Am I serving or self-serving?* That is why serving is costly, not convenient. Sacrifice is always a key ingredient!

Additionally, we cannot serve with a critical or insecure heart. The more insecure we are, the harder it is for us to serve, because we will always want others to serve us and meet our own needs. Only people with a secure heart can serve. Serving is forged out of a heart that is yielded to Jesus, and their identity is in Christ!

Bottom line: Serving is not an option. We need to be radical about serving others. Can you imagine the impact if thousands of Christians were to get passionate about serving their communities? Why shouldn't that revolution begin with us?

How to Use this Book

Serving takes an in-depth look at this core value and comes at it from 12 different angles as lived out by 12 different people. Their insights shed new light on this value and give us a model to follow.

You can read *Serving* individually or as part of a group. As part of a personal devotion time, you can gain insight as you read through each story and ponder on the "Training Time" questions at the end. Mentors can also use this book in a discipleship relationship, using the "Training Time" questions to step up to the next level. And small groups (huddles) can study the core value as a group to be prepared to sharpen each other with questions.

LIVING A PARADOX

Tony Dungy
Winning Super Bowl Coach of the Indianapolis Colts

Let your light shine before men, so that they may see your good works and give glory to your Father in heaven.
MATTHEW 5:16

Setting an example is not the main means of influencing another, it is the only means.
ALBERT EINSTEIN

One of the hardest obstacles for some people to overcome when it comes to accepting the Bible as infallible truth is the pervasive presence of paradox. The inclusion of these seemingly contradictory statements often plays tricks on the logical mind, even though the truth behind them can always be substantiated by neighboring Scriptures or by concepts revealed in more distant parts of God's Word.

Most of these paradoxical statements can be located in the four Gospels, where Jesus confounded the religious leaders of His time. For example, in Matthew 11:29-30,

Jesus tells us that we can find rest in working for Him. In Matthew 19:30, He says that the "first will be last, and many who are last will be first" (*NIV*).

Another one of Christ's more prominent paradoxes can be found in Matthew 16:25, where Jesus tells His disciples, "For whoever wants to save his life will lose it, but whoever loses his life because of Me will find it."

But spiritual paradoxes don't just exist in the Bible. There are living, breathing examples of this concept that can be readily found in the world around us.

Take for instance Tony Dungy. As head coach of the Indianapolis Colts, he has consistently turned conventional wisdom on its head. Consider the fact that Dungy always gets his players' attention without raising his voice or swearing. He's also a highly successful NFL coach and an equally successful family man.

And then there's Dungy's curious belief that to be an effective leader, one must actually be a servant to those he is leading. Dungy got this paradoxical idea from Matthew 20:26-27, where Jesus teaches that "whoever wants to become great among you must be your servant, and whoever wants to be first among you must be your slave."

"Ever since I've been in a leadership position, my focus has been the model of Christ as the servant-leader," Dungy says. "There are different ways to lead, but I've always felt that it's better if other people follow me because they want to follow, not because I've been put up there as the leader and they have to follow. To do that, you have to earn people's trust and their respect, and the way to do that is to show them you are there to help them. As coaches, that what's our job is—not necessarily to win a championship, but to help all the players, everyone in the organization, do their job as well as they can. That really is serving."

In an age when players work tirelessly to gain the approval of their coaches in order to earn starting positions and playing time, Dungy is a rare breed. He doesn't relish the role of leader as a means to attain self-gratification or a propped-up sense of respect. Instead, Dungy truly sees himself as a servant to his players and his coaching staff. His main objective is to make everyone around him better at what they do.

"To me, Christ's model really was the best," Dungy says. "I really try to, number one, be a role model and serve my team spiritually. I want to teach them as much as I can about football and how to be better players; but I also want to help them be good people, do well in the community and do well after football. So I try to present those things to them so that they can see that football isn't the end of the road. Therefore, I am hopefully serving them as individuals, serving their families and also serving them by giving everything I have to make them the best players they can be."

Colts' linebacker Tyjuan Hagler is certainly a believer in Dungy's methods. Hagler, also a professing Christian, has thoroughly enjoyed playing in Indianapolis since his rookie season in 2005. Hagler, a member of the Dungy-led Super Bowl XLI championship team, sees the serving nature of his coach even in the small things—such as Dungy's consistently laid-back demeanor and his approach to teaching through respectful personal interaction.

"I don't like it when coaches yell at me and cuss me out," Hagler says. "I like the coaches like him that just talk to you and break things down, like what you did wrong and what you need to do to correct it. I respect him so much for his coaching style, and I've got to thank God for bringing me to this team and Coach Dungy because that's the kind of coaching I respond better to."

Dungy was exposed to the concept of serving at a very young age. In fact, he was raised by two parents who exemplified such a lifestyle through their strong commitment to education in Jackson, Michigan, where Dungy was born and raised. Dr. Wilbur and CleoMae Dungy set a standard for their son that was further solidified by other close family members.

"[My parents'] attitude toward their jobs was that they were really helping people learn," Dungy recalls. "My grandfather was a minister, and I had two uncles who were ministers. That was their chosen way of serving and helping people understand the gospel and really doing it for other people's benefit. So I think I got to see that very early on just by watching my family."

Dungy also learned early on that serving isn't some complicated or even scary process that includes traveling to third-world countries or forsaking one's dreams for a life dedicated to full-time ministry. Instead, he has always had a balanced view of what being a servant truly entails.

"When I think of serving, I think of using the talents that the Lord has given you to help other people," Dungy simply states. "We always talk about using our talents for a purpose, but if you use them to help other people, I really feel like you're a servant.

"I just feel like I have that responsibility to model serving to others," he adds. "Some of the volunteer work I do, the charity work, is very satisfying; but it's satisfying because you feel like you've helped some other people— whether it's visiting a prison or a jail, whether it's helping out with Big Brothers or a Boys and Girls Club by giving someone an example. That part of it is important, and getting your satisfaction comes from feeling like you've helped someone, especially a young person."

That desire to help young people—especially young athletes—is a primary reason behind Dungy's lifelong support of Fellowship of Christian Athletes (FCA). He has seen time and again how one little spark can change another individual's outlook forever. Dungy believes that the ministry of FCA provides an invaluable opportunity for coaches to point young people toward Jesus. As far as Dungy is concerned, there is no better union than the one between athletics and ministry.

"I love the Bible, and the Bible really talks about how working for the Lord and athletics go hand in hand in a number of places," Dungy says. "Paul uses so many athletic metaphors because it's so fitting. It's hard work. It's not easy. You need determination. You have to be physically tough. You have to be mentally strong. And that to me is the image that I get of us as Christians and how we should be working for the Lord."

Dungy has served as a mentor in numerous organizations, such as Big Brothers, the Boys and Girls Club of America, All Pro Dad and, of course, FCA. But it's that daily routine of teaching his players both football skills and life skills that he continues to find most rewarding. And from experience, he knows just how important that relationship can be over the length of an athlete's career.

"So many players that we have," Dungy says, "when we ask them who the guiding force in their life was if they didn't have a dad, if they didn't have a mom who got you going, they all say it was a high-school coach or a junior-high teacher or someone in their life when they were growing up. It's a tremendous thing to be able to not only impact these players on the field in their sport but also impact them as people.

"Because of that responsibility of shaping these players spiritually as well as athletically, I think it's so important that we as coaches feed ourselves spiritually. We all go to clinics. We all go to camps. We understand our sport. But we need to understand what God wants us to do and to stay focused in our life so that we can not only tell our players what to do, we can show them. I think that's so critical."

When Dungy shares his philosophy on mentoring as part of the coaching process, he's not just reading from the pages of the latest bestseller on leadership, and he's not bringing a belief that he conjured up over years of experience. Instead, Dungy brings to the table a tried-and-true method of relational leadership that was modeled over 2,000 years ago by the ultimate servant-leader.

"Jesus had quite a few disciples, but there were 12 guys that He really poured Himself into," Dungy says. "Everything He did was to make those guys the best team they could be. At times, that involved teaching. At times, it involved Him being the example. At times, it involved one-on-one talks. For me, it's the same thing. I want my players to know that I'm not the one trying to be up front and get all the rewards of our business, but I'm really there to make them the best team they can be. That's going to involve working as hard as I can, spending hours studying the other team to get our game plans ready, and doing everything I can for them so that they can play well. But it's more than that. It's being involved, being there for them, being a sounding board for them and trying to help their families out. Anything that can help them get better at what they do, I'm here to provide that."

And that brings us back to this mind-boggling concept of paradox. Dungy's desire to serve others as a means to draw attention to his faith appears to send a conflicting message. But he takes his cue from Matthew 5:16, where Jesus says, "Let your light shine before men, so that they may see your good works." If you end the Scripture there, it obviously seems a bit odd that Jesus would encourage His followers to serve others just to get attention. That's why it's imperative to finish (and then digest) the rest of that verse, which goes on to say, "And give glory to your Father in heaven."

In other words, there is a greater purpose to serving than simply to help others. That is certainly a big part of the equation. God is, after all, a compassionate and caring God. But ultimately, we are to engage in a lifestyle of serving as a way to draw attention to God's mercy and grace and bring glory to His name. Even then, there is yet another purpose for serving that is often overlooked.

"I do think it's important for us to benefit other people, to help other people," Dungy says. "But I do think that in every station of life, we need role models. We, as Christians, need to model Christ and to show our young people what life is all about. Life is not all about taking, getting, receiving, taking advantage of opportunities that are presented to you, but life is also helping."

Jesus Himself proved this concept to be true during His ministry on Earth. As He healed the sick, fed the hungry, set the captives free and shared the message of eternal life with the masses that followed Him from town to town, Jesus did so knowing that His disciples were taking mental notes of everything He was doing.

"[Jesus] did some things in the course of His ministry strictly to show the disciples why He was here, what His

mission was; and He said, 'Let this be an example to you,'"
Dungy says. "He washed their feet so that they would understand what He was doing, why He was doing it and
what they were supposed to do as well. So I think that role
modeling was an important part of His ministry."

Not only did Jesus model serving for His disciples,
but He also modeled serving for every generation to follow. His actions were intended to set off a chain reaction
of selfless living among those who have chosen to bear
the name of Christ. And for Dungy, that means being
concerned with the physical and emotional needs of every
athlete on the Colts' roster.

"It's a big part of it, to show your players that you're
really here to make them better players," Dungy says.
"I tell them that all the time. That's our job as coaches.
It's nothing more than to help them get better. Yes, there
are some personal benefits that we're going to get out of
it; but really if we're in it for the personal benefits, we're
in it for the wrong reasons. You're a coach to help your
team and your players grow. When you see guys grow and
you see players get better on the field—you see them ma-
ture and gain confidence and all those things—that's
where you get all of your satisfaction: from knowing that
you have helped someone."

The light that shines before men through the witness
of a servant like Dungy can't be contained by the walls of
a football locker room. Jesus explains in Matthew 5:14 that
"a city situated on a hill cannot be hidden"—and neither

can the servant's light as it literally radiates the love of God to everyone within that individual's sphere of influence. Such is the case with the highly influential Coach Dungy.

"[Tony] lives out two great biblical commands—to love God and to love others," ESPN senior NFL analyst Chris Mortensen confirms. "There is no hypocrite in him. I can't say that about many people. I can't say that about me. . . . But every time I speak with Tony or I'm around him or I hear of other people's experiences with him, the more I want to be like him."

Despite the high praises that Dungy receives on a seemingly daily basis, his spirit of humility wards off any temptation to take even the shortest of ego trips. But he can't deny the joys that accompany a life of serving—especially when the fruits of his labor are born.

"For me, the biggest blessing comes down the road when someone says, 'Gee, that was really helpful to me,'" Dungy says. "It might not come right away. I know with the players, sometimes it comes 12 years later; and you're visiting with someone and they say, 'What happened in 1996 really made an impact on me, and here's how it helped.' There's no better feeling than that."

But according to Dungy, even more important than the blessings of serving is the call that every believer has received through the undeniable example of God's Son. "Christ said that [serving] was His mission," Dungy says. "That should tell us something."

TRAINING TIME

1. In what ways is Tony Dungy's life a living example of serving? Can you think of some other people, famous or not, who provide similar examples? What attributes do they possess and display? How do those people inspire you?

2. Who are some examples of serving in your life? How have they had an impact on you? How might others say that you are an example?

3. Read Matthew 5:16. What do you think Jesus meant when He said, "Let your light shine before men"? How do you think your good works can bring glory or attention to God?

4. Tony Dungy says, "Life is not all about taking, getting, receiving, taking advantage of opportunities that are presented to you, but life is also helping." Why do you think so many people in government, athletics, entertainment and society tend to live opposite of what Coach Dungy is suggesting?

5. What are some ways that you can be an example to your classmates, your teammates, your coworkers, your family members or your friends.

"FCA has been a big part of my life, not only growing up, but also now as an adult and as a coach. I think in our society, in our atmosphere today, athletics plays such a big part in especially our young people's lives. And in athletics—whether it's a coach, a teammate, a player, an official—we have a lot of opportunities to influence people. And we do influence people with sports. Unfortunately, many times, especially us as professional athletes and coaches, that influence isn't always positive. To me, that's where FCA comes in. It's where we can take the attractiveness of sports and turn it into a ministry and a way to share the gospel. And that's what FCA has done so well over its existence. . . . It's been a great vehicle for me to help other people come to know Christ. Sports in our society are so big. We have so many people who are involved—from very young people to coaches to fans. Sports seem to be a way to communicate across cultural barriers. I think we've got to use that to get the Christian message out, to get the gospel message out. We have a lot of opportunities to influence people, and we do influence people with sports. But unfortunately, many times—especially from us as professional athletes—that influence isn't always positive. But like FCA, we can take the attractiveness of sports and turn it into a ministry and a way to share the gospel."

—Tony Dungy

Empowered to Serve, Serving to Empower

Shaun Alexander
NFL Running Back

Go, therefore, and make disciples of all nations, baptizing them in the name of the Father and of the Son and of the Holy Spirit, teaching them to observe everything I have commanded you. And remember, I am with you always, to the end of the age.

MATTHEW 28:19-20

A teacher affects eternity; he can never tell where his influence stops.

HENRY BROOKS ADAMS

Shaun Alexander has always known there was something different about him. Even as a young 10-year-old boy, he sensed that his life would be far from ordinary. He began showing signs of above-average athleticism as a teenager and would go on to be one of the most prolific high-school football players ever produced by the state of Kentucky. And from there, he would achieve All-American status at the University of Alabama before making a massive impact in the NFL as the star running back of the Seattle Seahawks.

But it was more than his uncanny ability to run wild with the pigskin and score touchdown after touchdown that made Alexander special. It was his unusual desire to help others and serve the needs of anyone who crossed his path.

Up until his college career at the University of Alabama, Alexander's penchant for helping others was nothing more than an oddity. Then Alexander worked at his first Fellowship of Christian Athletes camp the summer before his junior year. That's when it all started to make sense.

"A lot of stuff happened at that FCA camp," Alexander says. "That's why I'm so involved with the FCA. I served that week but didn't know that it was God urging me on. I was doing these things by the grace of God, but when I saw the impact I had on those 10 boys that were my campers, I was like, *Wow! I'm giving them a service.* I get hyped off on providing a service for somebody. So that FCA camp was the first time where I had a natural setting of pouring out, and these boys were ready to receive. I just really enjoyed that. That's where the servant's heart really kicked in."

Alexander doesn't have to think too hard when considering where his interest in serving came from. His mother, Carol, exemplified generosity and compassion in ways that often defied logic.

"Let me tell you how powerful my mom was," Alexander says. "I honestly didn't know we were poor. I honestly didn't, because she was such a servant. She was always helping people financially. She was always driving people places.

She was always giving a good word to somebody. She was a servant to whoever had a need. I was just amazed by that."

Alexander was also blessed to have solid examples of serving away from home. Lucy and Lee Sellers provided a nurturing atmosphere for the young athlete while he was attending college in Tuscaloosa. Later on, he would grow to appreciate the heart of service exemplified by his wife, Valerie, and her family.

"Without seeing serving in my mom, seeing it from the Sellers family in Alabama or seeing it from my wife and her family, I think it would be understandable to hear the world say, 'You've got to think about yourself' and believe it," Alexander says. "We live in a selfish society where you've got to think about yourself. Society does not see you being a servant, and I think what happens is when you live your life and you see other people serve and you live your life as a servant, you learn how to do the greatest thing you could ever do, and that's walk with humility. That is the most powerful thing."

At that FCA camp, it was a powerful moment when the former NFL MVP realized that his desire to help people wasn't just a personality quirk or the nice thing to do—it was truly a calling for all of God's people. Not only did it answer some of his burning questions about life, but it also empowered him to act on that calling in a much more significant fashion.

"To do what God has called you to do is to be a servant," Alexander explains. "Sometimes that is simply pulling out a chair for someone. Sometimes it's opening up your arms to someone. Sometimes it's opening up your heart. It all comes out differently, but at the end of the day, it's about giving your life. That's what a servant does."

Once Alexander understood the purpose behind serving, he also came to another realization: "God's master plan is for everybody to have a chance to get to know Him," he says. "That is our purpose."

He cites a favorite Bible passage as further reinforcement of this master plan: "Do you not know that your body is a sanctuary of the Holy Spirit who is in you, whom you have from God? You are not your own, for you were bought at a price; therefore glorify God in your body" (1 Corinthians 6:19-20).

These words written by the apostle Paul to the church in Corinth may not seem like they are intended to address the issue of serving, but Alexander sees that last line—"therefore glorify God in your body"—as evidence that we have been created, not for our own pleasure, but to do the work of the Lord.

"Your body is for the Lord by honoring Him, praising Him, worshiping Him, leading others to Him, glorifying Him and teaching others about Him," he says. "So then how is the Lord for your body? Well, the Lord died for your sinful body. That's amazing."

For Alexander, the next step was to discover ways to live out that purpose and to step into the will of God. With two years of college eligibility left, he dove deeper into his work with FCA. In fact, his involvement with the organization's summer camps has become a regular staple of his commitment to serving and has afforded a never-ending supply of spiritual rewards.

"Over and over, it's the kids that you see changed," Alexander says. "I remember one of the kids' mothers wrote me a letter. She said, 'You know, I'm not really spiritual and I don't really know anything about that, but the last three years that you've been around my son has changed him. He is the most polite and upstanding young man. I just thank you for being a part of his life.' You've got young men, 14, 15 years old going to camp and then getting their whole household saved. You can't understand how God is using you for that. It just never makes sense to you. It's amazing. So those are the kinds of things that impact me."

But Alexander doesn't just serve through organized programs such as FCA, Communities in Schools, America's Foundation for Chess and the Matt Talbert Center; he also serves in ways that step outside the walls of conventional outreach, and takes a biblical approach that can be traced back to both the Old and New Testaments. Taking his cue from the likes of Eli, who mentored Samuel (as chronicled in the first chapter of 1 Samuel), and Paul, who mentored Timothy (as recorded in Acts and 1 and 2 Timothy), Alexander mentors 70 teenage boys who he refers to as his little brothers and says that he can't help but laugh when he thinks of how different they are now compared to how they were during their earliest meetings.

"I'm like, *God, I can't believe You used me to help save his soul*," Alexander says. "It's so much bigger than me. I mean, his soul is saved forever. God used me to impact that kid so much that he is now going to spend eternity in heaven. I even crack up when I see these boys mentoring other boys. It's crazy to me. So there is a joy and a refreshing feeling that comes over you when you start to recognize the impact of you impacting somebody else. It's better than anything that you can feel on your own."

According to Alexander, one of the biggest challenges most people face when it comes to serving is the difficult task of finding one's place. Those desiring to give of themselves often look to other servants for an idea of what they should do instead of seeking out unique opportunities that better reflect their abilities and personality traits.

"Everybody tries to put everything in a clean-cut box," Alexander says. "People might think that just because I mentor 70 kids, all of those kids have to mentor 70 kids, and now we're at 490 people. No, it does not work like that. That's where I think religion comes in, and also with religion our own selfish motives come in; and all of the sudden we're just all messed up. People don't even want to be a part of it. Instead, I would just tell people to find one friend and love on them every day."

Others struggling with the concept of serving may feel that it's too hard or too time consuming. Alexander points those individuals to the oft-sermonized passage found in Matthew 5:14-16. He is especially encouraged by verse 14, which points out, "A city situated on a hill cannot be hidden."

"Someone who is a light on a hill doesn't have to go find people," Alexander says. "They just live their life, and it's so attractive that people want to come and at least hear about it. So if I tell you, 'Go be a light on the hill,' you'd be like, 'Yeah! Is that all I have to do?' But if I told you, 'Hey, I want you to go and have eight Bible studies every day. I want you to call five other guys that you mentor every day,' then it's like, 'Oh my goodness.' That's hard."

Alexander also suggests that people should do the things they like to do and simply get together with people who share the same interests. After a while, opportunities to share the gospel with those who have yet to accept Jesus will come.

"That's serving," Alexander says. "You're being the part of the Body that God wants you to be. What's wrong is that most of us try to put a religious aspect on serving. But serving means you're going to do what the Master says. So now it's a choice. Do you accept the Master? Being a servant is walking in your calling—doing what the Master says. And if you're a servant, you don't have to worry about how or what."

Alexander also says that serving is circular in nature. The servant blesses a person in need, and then when the servant is in need, God blesses them back by providing them with a blessing of equal or greater value. His belief is substantiated by the words of Jesus in Luke 6:38: "Give, and it will be given to you; a good measure—pressed down, shaken together, and running over—will be poured into your lap."

"The Bible always says that when you give, it's going to come back to you," Alexander says. "I always believe that when you give to meet someone's need, you're going to get back whatever it is you need. That's how God works. We don't understand how great God is and how powerful He is and how He knows the plans for us way before we think we need something. So if you're saying 'God, use me. Choose me' all the time, then whenever you are in need, that person that you need, God's going to walk them right to you. It's a powerful thing when you know that's how God works."

Alexander continues to practice what he preaches. In 2005, he began working on a concept known as Club 37. This national accountability group will facilitate the mentoring and discipleship of young men from all walks of life who are striving to grow stronger in their faith and more focused on God. Alexander hopes to launch the organization's first camp series by 2010.

"It's going to be amazing," he says. "There's going to be a mentoring relationship where all of the men will mentor and all of the [boys] will be built up and loved so that eventually they can be mentors too. It's going to be all for Christ. We're going to set up something where we're going to teach every young man to become a fisherman and how to do it with a heart of serving and a spirit of excellence."

Another part of the process will be for the young men involved in the program to meet with each other once a year. Alexander says this concept goes back to his time at the FCA camps where he first experienced camaraderie and brotherhood with like-minded Christian young men.

"One of the most powerful things that young men can see is that we're all over this world, all over this country," he says. "It's powerful."

But without a strong element of faith, Alexander says that none of this is possible. It takes a childlike trust in God and His will for our lives to truly be able to move forward as the servants that He has called us to be.

"That to me is the definition of serving," says Alexander. "Even if I don't know how it's going to happen, I know that God told me to go, so I'm going. That could be speaking. That could be financial giving. That could be giving of time. That could be your body. That could be your mind. That could be watching TV or not watching TV. That could be listening to the radio or not listening to the radio. It all should go back to 'God, what is it You want me to do? I'm Your servant.' Jesus can call us friend. Amen to that. Thank You for calling me Your friend. Other people can be called ambassadors of the Kingdom. Amen. Thank You for calling me one of Your people. I love that. But we've got one title: servant. That's the only thing we can call ourselves. We can know that we're Jesus' friend. We can know we're ambassadors of the Kingdom. But when it comes to us and God, we only have one title, and that's servant."

Perhaps the most amazing aspect of serving is that service done with complete humility reaps the reward described by Jesus in Matthew 20:16: "So the last will be first, and the first last."

On the other hand, those who serve with selfish motivations or with a spirit of pride will face the brutal reality noted in Matthew 7:21-23: On the Day of Judgment, many who seemingly served God on Earth will be exposed as frauds. To those people, Jesus will say, "I never knew you! Depart from Me, you lawbreakers!" (v. 23).

That's a message Alexander says is imperative for all believers to understand.

"If you have any pride in you, you're in trouble," he says. "Every time you find yourself serving, you have to humble yourself. You have to humble yourself of the thought of who you are, the thought of, *Man, I shouldn't have to do this*. Don't ever think like that. And when you stay in that humble mode, then often you get to walk right into greatness."

TRAINING TIME

1. Can you think of a time when you realized God had a special plan for your life? How did that empower you and give you the confidence to move forward?

2. Read Matthew 29:19-20. Why do you think Jesus chose these as His last words to the disciples? What level of confidence do you think this final charge gave the disciples? How empowering is it to know that, as you step out to do God's will, Jesus is "with you always, to the end of the age"?

3. When has a teacher or mentor had a profound impact on your life? In what ways have you personally been able to mentor someone else? How did that mentoring process affect you? How did it impact the individual you were mentoring?

4. Read Matthew 7:20-23. What is your initial reaction to the harsh rebuke Jesus gives the religious leaders He is addressing? How is it possible for people to do good things for others and still be labeled "lawbreakers" on Judgment Day?

5. Read Matthew 20:16. How does this Scripture contrast with Jesus' words in the previous passage? When you live a humble life of service, what are some ways that you might "walk right into greatness" as Alexander suggests?

"I was floored by a speaker I heard recently. The guy told a story about people who had plans for their lives. These people had plans for their lives and then suddenly God says, 'I've got something for you to do.' Mary had plans. She was getting married to Joseph. She was planning who they were going to invite to the wedding and what she was going to wear. And then good old Gabriel shows up. He tells her she's going to get pregnant, and she's going to name the baby Jesus. It was overwhelming to Mary. This is how God does it. He says, 'Okay, Shaun, I know you're from Florence, Kentucky; but you're going to set up this mentoring program that's going to change the world, and you're going to be the MVP of the NFL.' I'm like, 'Right. We live in a basketball state, God. I think You're one state over.' But that's how I felt from the time I was 10, 11 or 12. I didn't know the timing of it, but I'm not surprised at where I am, because I felt these things were a calling way back then. When we have plans for our life, God brings somebody into our lives to tell us the direction He wants us to go in. Sometimes we don't understand it. Sometimes we do. But whether you understand it or not, God gives you the way. He shows you how it's going to happen. Then you have to choose."

—Shaun Alexander

At All Costs

Les Steckel
Fellowship of Christian Athletes President and CEO

Then He said to [them] all, "If anyone wants to come with Me,
he must deny himself, take up his cross daily, and follow Me. For whoever
wants to save his life will lose it, but whoever loses his life because of
Me will save it. What is a man benefited if he gains the whole world,
yet loses or forfeits himself?"

You must pay the price if you wish to secure the blessing.

Andrew Jackson

In 1954, a World War II veteran turned college coach named
Don McClanen sat across the table from Pittsburgh Pir-
ates general manager Branch Rickey. The meeting was the
result of a letter-writing campaign in which McClanen was
seeking face-to-face encounters with Christian athletes—
the people he considered to be heroes.

The five-minute meeting between the two men dragged
on for several hours and eventually birthed a revolution-

ary organization called the Fellowship of Christian Athletes. Rickey lent his name to fund-raising efforts while McClanen oversaw administrative efforts to get the ministry off the ground.

Shortly thereafter, McClanen left his coaching job at Eastern Oklahoma State College to focus on his passion for reaching young athletes with the gospel message by utilizing summer sports camps and school-based Bible study groups known as Huddles. McClanen and his wife, Gloria, made many sacrifices—mostly financial—as they balanced a desire to serve God with a responsibility to raise three children.

It was 51 years later in 2005 when a retired Marine and former NFL coach named Les Steckel became FCA's seventh president and CEO. By then, not only was FCA the largest interdenominational, school-based Christian organization in the United States, but the ministry was also exponentially increasing its international presence. The reality of FCA's overwhelming success had long since surpassed McClanen's wildest dreams.

So when Steckel—an active participant in FCA since 1972—was afforded the honored privilege to spend some quality one-on-one time with McClanen, now in his 80s, he was taken aback by the direction of their exchange.

"I'll never forget when Don McClanen looked at me in the eyes, and it was just the two of us standing there," Steckel recalls. "He said, 'Let me ask you something. Do you suffer?' I've never been asked that question in my entire life; and I looked at him and I said, 'Do I suffer?' And he said, 'Yes, do you have times of suffering?' And I said, 'I sure do.'"

No one had ever asked Steckel that question before, but he instinctively knew exactly the point McClanen was trying to make. He understood as well as anyone the fact that being in God's will often brings trials and tribulations and varying measures of emotional (and sometimes even physical) pain.

"When there is a cost to be paid, there is a moment where we have to stop and reflect," Steckel says. "If we're not suffering, then we may not be doing our job. Christ definitely suffered for us, so we need to suffer for Him."

No matter what the topic, Steckel will usually spend some portion of the conversation relating back to his 30 years of experience with the Marine Corps. The phrase "no pain, no gain" didn't originate in the military, but for anyone who has ever endured boot camp, the phrase could easily pass for the motto of any of its branches.

But surprisingly, it's not the pain Steckel tolerated that first comes to his mind. Instead, he thinks about how honored he was to serve his country with the Marines—particularly his tour in Vietnam—and how that service laid the foundation for his commitment to faith, family and FCA and helped him better understand the concept of serving.

"A Marine always says, 'Sir, reporting for duty, sir,'" Steckel relates. "Now, shouldn't we as Christians come to the Lord every day and say, 'Sir, reporting for duty, sir'? I really believe being a servant is reporting for duty on a daily basis."

Steckel also believes that a selfless approach to one's relationship with God ultimately results in the rewarding benefits that come from being right in the center of God's will. It's a concept he has always shared with his three children and anyone else who cares to listen.

"People always say, 'I feel called to this position'; and when you're called, it's exciting, but you also have to pay a price just like Christ paid the price," he says. "Oftentimes, I smile because we say that as believers in Christ, we want to be Christlike. But think about what Christ dealt with. First of all, Christ was rejected. So we get rejected a lot. There are times that we are scorned. We sacrifice. We have to surrender. We have to deny ourselves."

Steckel's interpretation of serving and sacrifice goes even deeper and is based on the following two verses found in Luke 9:24-25—which he believes holds one of the keys to understanding Christ's emphatic teaching of self-denial: "For whoever wants to save his life will lose it, but whoever loses his life because of Me will save it. What is a man benefited if he gains the whole world, yet loses or forfeits himself?"

There have been plenty of opportunities for Steckel to fall prey to the trappings of this world. He understands just how easily fame, fortune and power can trick people into thinking they've got it made when in reality they are

39

in danger of losing everything—even their very life. It was during his time in the coaching ranks that this reality first became clear.

Steckel was a college football assistant at the University of Colorado and then Navy before moving to the NFL, where he spent 23 of his 32 years as a coach. His stops have included San Francisco, New England, Denver, Houston, Tennessee, Buffalo and Tampa Bay. Steckel was also the head coach for the Minnesota Vikings in 1984 and coached in Super Bowls with the Patriots (1985) and Titans (2000).

"I admire the men I have worked with over the years who stay in close contact with their high-school buddies and their college buddies before they ever become a Hall of Fame football player," Steckel says. "Everybody wants to get your attention, and they give you plenty of affirmation to be your friend, and maybe they don't have a pure motive. I think those that God has given a platform where they can share their faith—like Tim Tebow or Tony Dungy—they have to be on constant guard against the secular world, against Satan and against self."

"It's very hard," Steckel continues. "People often rise to the top, and then they're suddenly no longer around. What happened to those people? You can think of athletes and coaches who have risen to the top quickly, and they've disappeared quickly. Like they say, it takes class to get to the top. It takes character to stay there."

Another key to having a servant's heart is humility. When his children still lived at home, Steckel says the entire family had a tradition of watching the movie *Jesus of Nazareth* every Easter. There was one scene in particular that had a tremendous impact on his understanding of serving.

"When I saw [the depiction of] Jesus washing the feet of His disciples, I couldn't imagine a more humbling experience," Steckel says. "Humility is an elusive thing. Once you think you've got it, you've lost it. I think we as Christians do a great job of faking it. We know how to say the right things. But there's a way of expressing yourself almost nonverbally, and the humility of a person can come through quickly. You don't see it too often, though, particularly in the athletic arena. But when you do, it's glaring; and when it's glaring, it can be mimicked and can sometimes be contagious."

In order to maintain humility, Steckel says that one must stay "grounded in the Word" and recognize that all talents and gifts come from God and are for the purpose of bringing Him glory. That understanding will consequentially move a person down a different track. Steckel is realistic, however, and knows that most people—especially those who don't have a relationship with Christ—often glaze over that principle and take the path of least resistance.

Steckel also warns that the athletes and coaches who do choose to serve God with their abilities shouldn't automatically expect to enjoy nothing but success on the playing field. But he does know from his personal experiences

41

that they can "have great satisfaction in knowing they're going about it the right way."

But according to Steckel, all of the humility in the world won't matter in the quest for a lifestyle of serving without first diving headlong into the example set by Jesus—the greatest servant to ever walk the earth. Sadly, many people—entire generations, in fact—not only fail to understand what serving means, but also can take on a completely skewed idea of what being a follower of Christ means.

"I've always felt like God brought His Son, Jesus, to this earth not only to save us and be our Savior but to serve us," Steckel says. "But you ask young people these days what it means to be a Christian, and you hear some shocking statements such as, 'When I don't swear or use profanity, I'm a Christian.' I've heard that. I've heard, 'If I go to church at least two times a month, then I'm a Christian.' People miss the boat completely."

Steckel looks no further than the symbolically charged Christmas story as proof that Jesus' mission was just as much about serving as it was about salvation.

"It's a paradox," he explains. "Here Jesus is the King of kings and the Lord of lords and the Son of the living God, and here He is being born in a cold, stinky cave. You talk about serving and sacrifice. And what about Mary who was put on a donkey? I think about the word 'labor.' Can you imagine being pregnant on a donkey going across a desert? I just think about the examples of Joseph and Mary and Jesus and the sacrifices they made and the humility of it all—the embarrassment of Mary initially, who gave birth to a child and claimed to be a virgin. I think about how God paints this picture."

It saddens Steckel when he realizes that most of the country and even most of the world celebrate Christmas, yet they never stop to consider the true purpose and meaning behind the story that ultimately conveys key ingredients of a Christian life—humility, serving and sacrifice.

"For the Christian, serving is a total surrender of your life to Jesus," Steckel says. "I think about how when Christ died on the cross, He said to us that His blood washed away our sins and whoever receives Him and believes in Him and serves Him will have eternal life. Now you can receive and believe and still get to heaven, but how can you not serve someone who has given their life for you so that you can have eternal life? There's got to be a love relationship. Why wouldn't you want to serve Him? So I've always said, 'Jesus gave His life for me. The least I can do is give my life for Him.'"

Still, so many who believe that Jesus died for them continue to struggle with the concept of total surrender and sacrificial serving. According to Steckel, the commitment to lay down one's selfish ambitions and prideful ways is to consider the words of the apostle Paul in Galatians 2:19-20: "For through the law I have died to the law, that I might live to God. I have been crucified with Christ; and I no longer live, but Christ lives in me.

The life I now live in the flesh, I live by faith in the Son of God, who loved me and gave Himself for me."

It's that kind of commitment that makes it possible for ordinary people with ordinary lives to perform extraordinary acts of service no matter the price that often must be paid—a price that might mean walking away from a high paying job, risking the loss of valued friendships or literally putting one's life on the line.

"I believe serving is a sacrifice," Steckel says. "I think it's a self-denying effort. For some it's easy. For others it's not. Serving is an interesting thing, particularly if you're serving as a missionary for Christ or an ambassador of Christ. We have so many great people in FCA who serve the Lord every day. There's a cost."

In fact, Paul takes the concept of serving a step further in 1 Corinthians 7:22-23, where he writes, "For he who is called by the Lord as a slave is the Lord's freedman. Likewise he who is called as a free man is Christ's slave. You were bought at a price; do not become slaves of men."

Interestingly, Paul chooses to use the word "slave" ("bondservant" in other translations), a word that for the individual who values freedom will likely invoke a decidedly negative response. But for Steckel, the imagery is both strong and, quite frankly, appealing, because it relates to the freedom that inherently comes from a subservient relationship with Christ.

"I think about how those men on those ships out at sea years ago were chained to the bottom of the ship's hull," Steckel says. "All they did was keep their eyes straight ahead and they just methodically kept rowing and rowing and rowing and at times were tortured and whipped. Being a bondservant, being a slave is something we're really called to do. We're called to be a servant. We're called to be a slave to Jesus."

In a society that promotes individual rights, personal freedoms and a smorgasbord of options, the idea that true happiness and fulfillment can come only through sacrifice and serving is foreign, to say the least.

At the end of the day, however, we must choose how much we are willing to sacrifice in order to fulfill the purpose and calling God has for our lives. We have the ability to accept the call to serve or to reject it. And even when we say yes to His will, we are continually faced with choices. Paradoxically, we still have freedom despite our role as slaves of the Kingdom.

"I really believe that today we can all be the quarterback," Steckel says. "God gives us the free will to make those calls and to audible at the line of scrimmage. But when we do, we have to recognize that what we're trying to do is score for Him and bring Him glory, not ourselves. So when we make those decisions, we have what I refer to as the power of choice. We have the choice to serve or not serve. We have the choice to make that decision to serve or go another direction."

TRAINING TIME

1. Read Philippians 1:29. How does that Scripture change your perception of what it means to live the Christian life? What are some ways that you might be required to suffer for the cause of Christ?

2. Read Luke 9:23-25. In verse 23, what do you think Jesus meant when He instructed His disciples to take up their cross daily and follow Him? How do verses 24 and 25 remind you of people seeking fame and fortune in today's world? How is it possible to lose your life and save it at the same time?

3. The lasting effects of slavery in America caused strife and contention for hundreds of years, yet Steckel argues that we are to become slaves to Christ. Read 1 Corinthians 7:22-23. How does that passage back up Steckel's claim? What is the difference between freedom in Christ and the kind of freedom the world offers? Which is more attractive, and why?

4. Steckel says, "We have the choice to serve or not serve." What are some things that might keep you from serving? How do you feel when you've chosen not to serve as compared to how you feel after you've served?

5. Read Romans 8:16-18. What are the benefits that accompany the sacrifice of service? How does this passage encourage you to embrace that lifestyle?

"I'm married to the most wonderful servant I've ever known on the planet Earth—my wife, Chris, who absolutely loves to serve. For me, serving is a little difficult at times, I confess; but it's so simple for her. She would rather serve somebody other than herself any day of the week, and she gets true joy out of it. One night in 1990, when I was out of work, she was busy fixing dinner. As we sat down to eat, she couldn't even finish her meal. She had to quickly put on her topcoat and head to the church for a committee meeting. After she left, I had time to feed the children, clean up the kitchen, wash the dishes, sweep the floor, clean off the table, give the children their baths, put them in their pajamas, read them stories, say prayers and put them all in bed. For my wife who receives love by being served, that was the ultimate serving that I had done for her in 16 years of marriage. When she came home and saw that the kitchen was immaculate, the tables were clean and our three kids were asleep in bed, it was the quickest I've ever seen the fire lit in the fireplace, the lights dimmed and the soft music turned on. I served the servant, and it was a way of expressing admiration and appreciation. Needless to say, she felt it; and now I've learned to do that more often."

—Les Steckel

True Leadership

Pat Williams
Senior Vice President of the Orlando Magic

Whoever wants to become great among you must be your servant,
and whoever wants to be first among you must be your slave;
just as the Son of Man did not come to be served, but to serve,
and to give His life—a ransom for many.

MATTHEW 20:26-28

Everybody can be great . . . because anybody can serve.

DR. MARTIN LUTHER KING, JR.

From his study of leadership, Pat Williams is convinced that there are seven sides to being an effective leader. The first is vision, or the ability to see down the road. Next is a gift for communicating that vision. Williams also says that people skills are an important leadership trait. This includes a true heart for people and a genuine interest in their lives. The next three qualifications are character, competence and boldness.

As the senior vice president of the NBA's Orlando Magic, Williams certainly has built a lengthy career by displaying a high level of acumen in those six areas.

But it's the seventh characteristic that he says makes the better-than-average leader a great leader.

"There are many six-sided leaders out there, and they are doing a good job," Williams says. "But to be a leader for the ages—one who will never be forgotten, a leader who will go down in the history books—the seventh side of leadership must be there. That is called a servant's heart, though I like the verb form better—a serving heart. When a man or woman in leadership has a serving heart, that person will always be remembered."

Over the course of history, there have been many seven-sided leaders. Some notable figures that immediately cross Williams's mind include the Old Testament hero Joseph, along with such other historical figures as William Wilberforce, Dr. David Livingstone, Dr. Albert Schweitzer, Ghandi, Mother Teresa, Dr. Martin Luther King, Jr., President Ronald Reagan, Billy Graham, John Wooden and Senator Robert Kennedy.

And then there's R. E. Littlejohn.

If you've never heard of Littlejohn, don't feel bad. Williams didn't know who he was either until 1965, when he went to work for the Philadelphia Phillies' farm club in Spartanburg, South Carolina, a team owned by Littlejohn. As a budding executive and rookie general manager, Williams immediately became enamored with the wealthy businessman who made his money in oil transportation.

Previously, Williams (a seven-year Army veteran) had spent two years as a minor-league catcher with the Phillies, preceded by a successful stint playing college baseball at Wake Forest, where he was part of the 1962 Atlantic Coast Conference Championship team and was later inducted into the Wake Forest Sports Hall of Fame.

Despite the densely compacted life experience Williams brought to Spartanburg, it was nothing compared to the invaluable lessons he would learn from Littlejohn—his first true leadership mentor.

"Mr. Littlejohn had an enormous impact on me," Williams recalls. "He modeled servant leadership in front of me every day. He was wealthy and successful, but you never would have known it. People gravitated to him. He had a marvelous quality called wisdom, and people sought out that wisdom. He had a gentle, loving spirit. He loved the Lord and genuinely cared for people and put other people first. I just saw him modeling serving leadership. It left a huge impression on me."

In late February 1968, Williams committed his life to Christ at the age of 27. Shortly thereafter, his career would take a trip on a fast track to success that included earning a master's degree at Indiana University and a doctorate from Flagler University. Williams was also eventually inducted into the Sports Hall of Fame in Delaware, the state in which he was raised.

Yet the faith he embraced—thanks to Littlejohn's example—helped him come to terms with the true meaning of life. And the "enormous change" that Williams experienced that day allowed him to see things from a completely different perspective.

"Up to that point, everything had been about me," he admits. "Then I realized that once Christ comes into your life, it's others first. That's how He lived His life, and that's the model He left for us. So I think at that point you really begin to change in your priorities."

After his stint within the Phillies' organization, Williams spent the next three years doing similar work with the Minnesota Twins. Then in 1968, he made the move to the NBA, where he's been ever since. Williams's stops have included Chicago, Atlanta and Philadelphia, where he worked with the 1983 World Champion 76ers.

In 1987, he cofounded the Orlando Magic and helped lead them to the NBA finals in 1995. The following year, a prominent national magazine named Williams one of the 50 most influential people in NBA history. Perhaps that honor had something to do with the fact that 23 of his teams have made the playoffs and 5 of them have reached the finals.

Williams has also been involved in high-profile trades that involved the likes of Pete Maravich, Julius Erving, Moses Malone and Penny Hardaway. He has also been a part of staffs that have drafted Charles Barkley, Shaquille O'Neal, Maurice Cheeks, Andrew Toney, Darryl Hawkins and Dwight Howard. Williams gave several prominent coaches—including Chuck Daly and Matt Guokas—their first coaching positions, and 12 of his former players have become head coaches while 17 former players have become assistant coaches.

Beyond his success in the sports world, Williams has also become known as one of the nation's most popular motivational speakers and authors. But perhaps even more impressive is his active lifestyle, which boasts weight training and running. In fact, he has completed 38 marathons over the past decade, including 10 successful attempts at the Boston Marathon. On top of that, Williams participates in a Major League Baseball fantasy camp where he has caught for such Hall of Fame pitchers as Bob Gibson, Gaylord Perry, Tom Seaver and Phil Niekro.

Yet nothing speaks to Williams's success quite like his role as a devoted husband and father. He says it was that weighty responsibility that vastly increased his knowledge of serving.

"After I became a father was another huge turning point," Williams says. "Our family kept growing and growing and growing, and we ended up with 19 children. I certainly learned in that world that you're constantly in a serving position. Now it's starting again with the grandchildren."

Of Williams's and wife Ruth's 19 children, 14 are adopted from four countries. While they are now all adults, there was one point in the family's fascinating history during which 16 of the children were teenagers at the same time. This storybook angle has drawn attention from such national publications as *Sports Illustrated*, *Reader's Digest*, *Good Housekeeping* and the *Wall Street Journal*. Williams's family has also been featured on such TV programs as *The Maury Povich Show*.

Williams has also learned about serving leadership by teaching an adult Sunday School class at First Baptist

Church of Orlando. He also says that his longtime partnership with Fellowship of Christian Athletes has been another integral part of his public life. While in Philadelphia, he established the local FCA chapter there during the 1968-69 season. When he moved to Chicago, he helped facilitate the FCA's burgeoning work there. Upon moving to Atlanta, Williams plugged into a pre-existing FCA chapter before spending another 12 years with the 76ers, where he remained a key player in the organization's growth.

"Over the last 40 years, many of the most rewarding experiences have been with the Fellowship of Christian Athletes," Williams says. "FCA involvement over the past four decades has probably been as fulfilling to me as anything that I've done while serving the Body of Christ."

Williams says other educational opportunities have come from spending significant time with some modern examples of the serving leader. Legendary college basketball coach John Wooden and Orlando Magic ownership chairman Rich DeVos are two men in particular that Williams sites for their exemplary public and private service. In fact, he was so inspired by their examples, he wrote books about both men.

To this day, Coach Wooden—who coached the UCLA Bruins to an unprecedented 10 consecutive NCAA titles—continues to amaze Williams. "John Wooden is the most successful coach of all time," he states. "He's set records that will never be touched. But Coach Wooden is a servant. He has a caring heart. He's got a great love for other people, and he's never too busy for anybody. He's never too important for anybody. It's a beautiful thing to watch."

Another one of Williams's favorite examples of serving leadership is the world-famous evangelist Billy Graham. He has been privileged to speak at two of Graham's crusades but has been even more blessed to see firsthand what kind of selfless humility it takes to truly have a servant's heart.

"I do a radio show in Orlando every week, and I once interviewed Ruth Graham, who is Billy Graham's youngest daughter," Williams recalls. "She had just written a book, and I was interviewing her about the book. Toward the end of the show I asked her just to reflect on her famous father. I asked Ruth to share some insight into her dad and why he was unique. Ruth Graham, in that wonderful North Carolina drawl, said, 'My daddy knows who he is— a flawed human being. In Daddy's mind, he's still just a farm boy from North Carolina.' And I thought that just captured it beautifully."

His impression of Graham was solidified even further when he traveled to Charlotte, North Carolina, where he was able to visit the Billy Graham Library and grounds, which were opened to celebrate the minister's storied life. "You go through the barn and his boyhood home," Williams describes. "Here's probably as famous an American as we've ever had in the past 100 years, and yet he just views himself as a country preacher from Charlotte. I like that quality very much. That truly appeals to me."

As impressive as Williams's list of mentors might be, in his opinion there is only one person who can be described as "the epitome of the serving leader." Williams is especially struck by the simple instruction and humility expressed by Jesus in Matthew 20:26-28. Yet even Williams's closest friends and confidantes had a hard time grasping this particular teaching that flies in the face of conventional wisdom and challenges human nature's deeply ingrained selfishness.

"Jesus had a very interesting philosophy," Williams says. "This is my version of the Scriptures, but basically He said to His disciples, 'You want to be great? Want to get to the top? Want to be number one? I'll tell you how. Go out and serve other people.' I can just imagine how shocked they were when they heard that, because they were probably no different than anybody today. 'That's not what it says in this motivational book I'm reading, Jesus.' But that was His approach."

The ultimate example of Jesus' serving heart can be found in Matthew 26 (see also Mark 14 and Luke 22), in which Jesus went to a place called Gethsemane to pray with His disciples. He knew that the time of His death was near. In those moments, Jesus struggled with His humanity like never before. He cried out, "My Father! If it is possible, let this cup pass from Me. Yet not as I will, but as You will" (Matthew 26:39).

Even after enduring grueling and torturous experiences on the way to His crucifixion, Jesus still remained true to His serving spirit as He hung from the cross. In

Luke 23:34, He prayed, "Father, forgive them, for they do not know what they are doing."

Jesus' contrite, forgiving spirit pales in comparison to the cutthroat leadership that is typical of the management style often found in modern-day corporate America. Williams, however, believes that the current corporate philosophy is slowly but surely being phased out in exchange for the biblical alternative.

"So much of the time we're presented with leadership being a dominant force, overwhelming people or browbeating them or intimidating them," Williams says. "But I don't really think that's leadership. I think that's called assault and battery. I would suggest that the days of Attila the Hun leadership are over, as are the General Patton days. They're gone. And as leaders, we've got to avoid the temptation to adapt that style, because in the long run it demeans people and degrades people."

Williams says that leaders who feel the need to use domination and intimidation in order to get others to follow them are usually bound by pride and selfishness. Sometimes that attitude is actually born out of the individual's struggle with self-worth and inferiority. Other times, it simply boils down to entitlement issues that infiltrate the soul like a ravenous cancer.

"We're always battling that," Williams says. "So many men and women, when they get promoted into a leadership position—they become the head coach or they become the athletic director or they become the CEO or the high-school principal—so many cannot handle an overflowing cup. They begin to inhale all of this stuff. And let's face it, with leadership there are some good things. There are some perks. Leaders get parking privileges and golf-club memberships and executive washroom keys and some really good stuff. But that good stuff has ruined more leaders than anything else. When we really begin to think that by divine right, this is all mine, that's the beginning of the end. Any sense of a humble spirit is obliterated."

The Bible is clear about what happens to leaders (or anyone for that matter) who allow selfishness and pride to control their actions. Proverbs 16:18 tells us that "pride comes before destruction, and an arrogant spirit before a fall." Isaiah 2:11 prophecies that "human pride will be humbled, and the loftiness of men will be brought low."

Yet those seeking to be serving leaders can find solace in truths found in passages such as Proverbs 11:2, which suggests that "when pride comes, disgrace follows, but with humility comes wisdom." And along with that wisdom, the recognition of those golden opportunities to serve others can be much more easily found.

"At the end of the day, that's really what you'll be remembered for—what you contributed to other people's lives," Williams says. "That triggers my speaking and my writing. Every time I write a book or deliver a message, I want it to make a difference in people's lives. To get feedback later, you can't put a price tag on that. It's still the most uplifting experience I get in life."

TRAINING TIME

1. Pat Williams names seven keys to successful leadership. Name some people (living or dead, famous or not famous) who you think embody the qualities of a great leader. Which of those individuals would you say exhibit signs of the serving leader?

2. Read Matthew 20:20-28. In this story, how did James and John (and their mother) perceive the benefits of being a leader? How did Jesus' teaching on leadership contrast in comparison?

3. Read Matthew 26:39. Can you describe a time when you wanted God to pass the cup of responsibility to someone else? How did you gather the strength to carry on with God's will for your life? What was the end result of that sacrifice?

4. Read Proverbs 16:18. What does this Scripture tell you about people who allow pride to keep them from a life of service? Can you describe some times in which your pride caused you to fall?

5. Read Proverbs 11:2. What benefit can be found for those who choose humility over pride? In what ways might wisdom help you to become a better leader? How can wisdom lead you to more opportunities for serving?

"I was in Kansas City, speaking at a leadership conference, and I had the morning off, so I decided to go for a jog. I ended up at the corner of 40th and Main, and I noticed a monument across the street. I've always been a sucker for monuments and historical markers, so I jogged to the other side to get a closer look. The monument was dedicated to Major Murray Davis. He was a Kansas City native who was killed in Exermont, France, on September 28, 1918, during World War I. On one side of the monument it read, 'A kindly, just and beloved officer, wise in counsel, resolute in action, courageous unto death.' And on the other side it read, 'Seriously wounded, he refused to relinquish his command until mortally wounded he fell leading his comrades to victory. His last words were "Take care of my men." ' And I thought, He got it. He understood that whole issue of being a serving leader. . . . When people know that their leader is truly there to serve them and cares about them as human beings—not just as producers, but as real people—that can change the heart of any organization."

—Pat Williams

PRIDE FIGHTER

Tim Tebow
NCAA Quarterback and Heisman Trophy Winner

Make your own attitude that of Christ Jesus, who, existing in the form of God, did not consider equality with God as something to be used for His own advantage. Instead He emptied Himself by assuming the form of a slave, taking on the likeness of men. And when He had come as a man in His external form, He humbled Himself by becoming obedient to the point of death—even to death on a cross.

PHILIPPIANS 2:5-8

He that is proud eats up himself: pride is his own glass, his own trumpet, his own chronicle; and whatever praiseth itself but in the deed, devours the deed in the praise.

WILLIAM SHAKESPEARE

Tim Tebow, the 2007 Heisman Trophy winner and member of the 2006-07 National Championship Florida Gators, wasn't supposed to be a superstar quarterback. In fact, if his mother's, Pam Tebow's, doctors would have had their way, his birth would have been permanently postponed.

In early 1987, Pam and her husband, Bob, were serving as missionaries in the Philippines. Pam was pregnant with

Tim when she contracted amoebic dysentery—an intestinal infection caused by the presence of parasites in food or drink. Because of the strong possibility that the drugs she needed to combat the infection would endanger the unborn child, Pam Tebow's doctors strongly suggested that she have an abortion. After all, in their opinion, if the baby survived, it would very likely suffer from severe disabilities.

Every negative report was proven wrong on August 14, when a perfectly healthy boy was welcomed into the world. Tebow lived in the Philippines with his family until he was three years old, but his unusual life was just beginning. In Jacksonville, Florida, he and his four siblings were all home-schooled by their mother, despite the fact that the practice was very uncommon at the time.

"I was the youngest, so for me it was pretty normal being home-schooled," Tebow says. "But when my parents starting home-schooling, it was an odd thing. No one really knew about it. They didn't always get praise for doing it, and some people frowned upon it. But my parents figured, 'Hey, there are some things we want our children to learn that are more important than academics.' It's not that they weren't stressing academics, which they were, but they were emphasizing more biblical things and character more than anything else. That's why my parents chose to home-school—so that we would learn to praise God and have character before learning our ABCs or how to add. I'm thankful to my parents for doing that and instilling those things into me and my siblings."

One of the persistent knocks against home-schooling has been the lack of extracurricular activities available to students not attending traditional public or private institutions. But in Florida, that changed in 1996 when legislation was passed allowing home-schooled students the opportunity to participate in local high-school sports and other competitive activities.

Tebow was showing signs of athleticism, and the new law allowed him to play football at Trinity Christian Academy in Jacksonville, where he was a linebacker. But his desire to play quarterback in a passing offense caused him to search out other options. That search led him to Nease High School in Ponte Vedra Beach, where he and his mother moved into an apartment in the same county to gain eligibility. By his junior season, Tebow was on every major college's recruiting list. His status was solidified when as a senior he led his team to the state title. He was also named to the prestigious All-State team. Tebow's exploits as a home-school prodigy eventually led advocates in the neighboring state of Alabama to create the Tim Tebow Bill, which would give its home-school athletes the same rights to compete on local high-school sports teams.

When others try to heap praise on Tebow for the inspiration he has provided to so many people at such a young age, he is quick to give credit to his serving-minded parents, who diligently taught him about Jesus. But ultimately, Tebow says, he had to come to that life-changing decision on his own.

"I was blessed to grow up in a Christian home," he says. "We always went to church every Sunday, but it never really clicked for me until a few years down the road. I realized when I was still pretty young that even though I was a pretty good person, I was a sinner too. Maybe I wasn't doing things that were superbad in the eyes of the world, but I was still a sinner, and I needed a Savior. I realized that Christ died on the cross for my sins, and if I put my trust in Him, I'd have eternal life in heaven. I knew I needed that. I needed a Savior, and Jesus Christ was knocking on the door of my heart. So I received Him into my heart, and He's there with me today."

When it came time for Tebow to choose where to play college football, his faith was a strong component in the decision-making process. He eventually chose the tradition-rich University of Florida, which touted the 1996 National Championship and numerous NFL alumni, including Jack Youngblood, Cris Collinsworth, Emmitt Smith, Ike Hilliard and Jevon Kearse, as well as Heisman Trophy winners Steve Spurrier and Danny Wuerffel.

His choice paid off almost immediately. As a freshman, he played a significant part in the Gators' second BCS National Championship team during the 2006-07 campaign. Although Tebow was a backup quarterback to senior Chris Leak, he made major contributions as a dual-threat option and was called upon regularly in several key moments—including two touchdown passes and a rushing touchdown against Southeastern Conference opponent LSU and a touchdown pass and a rushing touchdown against

Ohio State in the 2007 BCS National Championship game.

Tebow took the reigns as quarterback as a sophomore in 2007 and proceeded to break multiple SEC and NCAA records. He became the first NCAA player to rush for 20 touchdowns and pass for 20 touchdowns in the same season. Tebow's ability to run and throw at equally high levels of proficiency earned him numerous accolades, including the Maxwell Award, the Davey O'Brien Award and consensus First Team All-American honors.

He topped off his second season by becoming the first sophomore to win the prestigious Heisman Trophy, generally recognized as the ultimate prize in all of college football. Yet amazingly, Tebow has done his best to deflect much of the praise and redirect it elsewhere.

"I am not out there playing for myself," Tebow says. "I love the game, but I am playing for the Lord Jesus Christ. I am going out there and loving the game and giving everything I have 100 percent and hoping that they can see the love of Christ through me."

Some might assume that Tebow's humility has more to do with his laid-back personality or perhaps his humble beginnings in a missionary family. But there's so much more to his selfless style of leadership than meets the eye. In fact, Tebow looks at his role as a high-profile quarterback the same as any other position in life.

"I think anything can be a ministry, especially football, because you have a platform," Tebow says. "You have 100 guys in the locker room with you every day. But more importantly than that, you have 1,000 kids looking up to you and a lot of people all across the country—you have the opportunity and platform to share with them, and to not take advantage of that would be a big mistake."

According to the University of Florida media relations department, Tebow has received more than 200 requests for appearances and speaking engagements since his on-campus arrival. These inquiries have ranged from a diverse list of organizations including churches, youth ministries, schools and civic groups across the southeastern United States. Tebow credits Fellowship of Christian Athletes for much of his current understanding of what ministry looks like. He attended FCA events with his father and brothers as a five year old and has been involved ever since. His brother Robbie Tebow, in fact, is the organization's area director over North Florida.

Even with such a solid supporting cast of family members and spiritual mentors, Tebow says playing football on such a large platform presents its challenges. Thankfully, the wisdom that has been imparted into his life thus far provides an escape from the temptation of letting pride, self-importance and out-of-whack priorities take control.

"It's tough," Tebow admits. "You love a game like football. You love to play it. You love everything about it. It's tough once you've done it for so long to not let it become the number one thing in your life, not to let that become your god. You always have to realize that there are more important things than playing football or winning games or throwing a touchdown pass. It's more about how you're treating people and your relationship with Jesus Christ. Are you giving Him the honor and glory for everything? It takes staying in His Word and staying humble and realizing that there are things that are more important than football. I think that's the number one thing for me."

Tebow has also benefited from the example of boldness, courage, strength and humility that his father has set for him. Having those attributes engrained into his heart, mind and soul has given him a unique understanding of the difficult concept of serving.

"To me, serving means putting others' needs in front of your needs," Tebow says. "It's doing what you can to take care of other people before you focus on your own wants and needs. I learned the biblical principles of serving when I was very young, especially seeing how my parents have given of their time, life and money to serve others around them."

Although Tebow was only three years old when he and his family moved back to Florida from the Philippines, he has been privileged to make several trips back to the heavily populated islands located in Southeast Asia. The experience has been both positive and educational.

"Meeting all of those different people who have nothing and are poor gave me an appreciation for what my family and I have," Tebow says. "It provided me with the perspective of taking nothing for granted. It also allowed me to see the effect that I could have on those people.

For some, the belief in Christ is all that they have and is much more important than money or material possessions."

Tebow believes that his experience has also helped him to not get caught up in all the stress that is involved in being a leading college quarterback. "Going to the Philippines with my dad and being at the orphanage and hanging out with the kids help keep me from getting too wrapped up in what's going to happen on fourth down," Tebow says. "Instead, it lets me realize how much of a blessing it is to have the athletic ability to go out there and play football. That takes a lot of pressure off. It lets you go out there and enjoy playing and have fun."

Off the field, Tebow has quickly earned the reputation of having an eager willingness to serve the community, though, he admits, he must constantly be on the lookout for the enemies of serving, which include personal ambition and pride. "I think pride is an issue for everybody," Tebow says. "It is always an issue for everybody. You have to stay humble and realize that God gave you your abilities, and He can take them away at any time. You just have to be thankful for them and try to use the talents that God gave you to influence as many people as you can."

Long before Tebow was a Heisman Trophy winner and an All-American, his ministry-focused parents laid a solid foundation that has since helped keep his pride in check. "It's funny, but when I was very young in t-ball and stuff, my parents would never let me tell anyone how many home runs I hit or how many touchdowns I scored," he recalls.

"They would never let me say it until the other person would ask me. So when I was five or six or seven, I'd always want to be like, 'I just hit three homeruns,' but I was never allowed to tell them until they asked me. That was a lesson I learned when I was really young. God blessed me with athletic ability, and that can be taken away in an instant. So I've just been thankful for it and never let myself get too proud. Just because you play football doesn't make you any more special than anybody else.

"I like to think that I've been able to use many of the valuable lessons that my parents have taught me. I am fortunate to have family members, coaches and teammates around who can help me stay focused on the right things for me to be successful. For me, every day includes four things: God, family, academics and football—in that order. And that's thanks to my family. Seeing how my parents have raised us and provided everything we can possibly need is a comforting feeling. I have been so blessed to have an amazing support group, and knowing how passionate they are about God and us kids has inspired me."

Ironically, Tebow says that being a high-profile athlete actually has made serving easier. That's because opportunities to spend time with others and to share the gospel with them are always lurking around the corner. But Tebow still remains careful to convey a message of humility and selflessness to the various groups he addresses. He passionately points others to Jesus, who, according to Philippians 2:7, "emptied Himself by assuming the form of a slave, taking on the likeness of men."

"Jesus was the best leader ever, so you can learn everything about leadership from Him," Tebow says. "Seeing how He died on the cross for you and just learning from the best leader ever, you can just take that and apply it to your life in every aspect—not just leadership but also how you handle talking and interacting with people."

Tebow can't predict his future, although most NFL Draft prognosticators seem to think he will have a long professional career ahead of him. One thing is for certain: Finding ways to reach out and serve others will always be a part of his life. That includes working with his father's ministry—the Bob Tebow Evangelistic Association—and assisting more than 40 national evangelists working in the Philippines.

"After football, I'd like to be involved again in the ministry in some way," Tebow says. "The Philippines are pretty special to me, and every year in high school up until college, I've been part of a group my dad would take there. It is a great experience. We go into medical clinics, hospitals, prisons, market places and schools. You preach and help out. We go to the orphanage and a lot of things like that. It's a great experience. I love going every year, and I can't wait until I go back.

"The Philippines is definitely in my future after football. When you come back home, you're grateful for everything that God's given you, and you see how blessed you are."

TRAINING TIME

1. Tim Tebow's story is wrapped in many elements of humility, including the circumstances of his birth, his early life in the Philippines and his subsequent home-schooling background. What parts of your life story might help you to remain humble in the midst of personal success?

2. Tebow says, "Maybe I wasn't doing things that were superbad in the eyes of the world, but I was still a sinner and I needed a Savior." Read Romans 3:23. When did you first realize the truth found in that passage? How did it change your life?

3. After winning the 2007 Heisman Trophy, Tebow could have easily given in to prideful thinking, but instead he chose to remain humble. Read Isaiah 2:11. How can you keep an attitude of humility regardless of the amount of success you achieve? What are the dangers that often accompany pride?

4. Read Philippians 2:5-8. In what ways did Jesus display humility when He was on Earth? How might the average person have acted differently if he or she possessed the same divine heritage?

5. How does eradicating pride from your life make it easier to serve God and others? What are some ways that you might be able to rid your heart of pride?

"Because of my faith, I receive a lot of requests to speak to different organizations. I like to do as many as I can. During the summer of 2007, I had the opportunity to speak at the state prison in Union County. I got to get up and preach. The people there don't have a lot to look forward to, and they don't have a positive outlook on things. I told them that everyone looks at them like they are nothing, and I told them that they are no different than I am, except they made a bad choice. That doesn't make them any worse of a person, and God doesn't love them any less. I let them know that because of their actions, there are consequences, but God wants them to go to heaven. There were people in there for all sorts of things. There were murderers and drug lords. I saw these guys break down and cry. I gave them an invitation to accept Jesus Christ and change the way they were living. In the two prisons I spoke at, 195 guys came forward. I held their hands and prayed with them. The security guys told them they weren't allowed to get close to me, but I wasn't worried about it. I felt like I was doing what God wanted me to do, so it was safe."

—Tim Tebow

THE ACT OF WORSHIP

Ruth Riley
WNBA Forward

And Jesus answered him, "It is written:
Worship the Lord your God, and serve Him only."

LUKE 4:8

The New Testament is about Jesus coming and laying his life down
and preferring other people. I think the whole essence of worship is
about that. It's about laying down our lives, about feeding the poor,
about reaching out to others, which is the essence of what happened
when Jesus came. He fulfilled everything. It meant God could be real
to mankind in a personal way and because of that we can understand
what it is to worship him and have a relationship with Him.

TIM JUPP OF DELIRIOUS?

If you want to know how much an athlete loves his or her particular sport, find out about that athlete's daily routine. The basketball player might shoot hundreds of jump shots and free throws. The baseball or softball player will likely spend an entire afternoon in the batting cage. The weightlifter can probably be found doing reps in the gym before and after class. The cross-country runner can usually be spotted jogging along the city's sidewalks.

Why do these athletes discipline themselves to such regimented and demanding workouts? They put in the time because they are driven to succeed. They are driven to be the best. And, ultimately, it's this simple: They have a passion for athletic competition.

Ruth Riley can relate. She too is very passionate about her sport of choice—basketball. So for the WNBA star, working out during the off-season, staying late after practice to work on post moves, or watching a game film when everyone else has called it a day is certainly not a foreign concept. Going that extra mile and a half is fueled by passion, even when the hard work is far from fun.

It kind of reminds Riley of her days on the farm back in Macy, Indiana, where she and her brother and sister were raised by their mother, Sharon. She believes that her strict upbringing kept her on the straight and narrow, even when she fought the disciplinarian oversight as an older teenager. Riley also explains that "going to church was not optional," and it was serving in the mundane things that taught her invaluable lessons that would fully apply to her life a few years later.

"We would stay late after church and vacuum or help out by doing other things," Riley says. "And there were times when I'd think, *Gosh, I really don't feel like doing this right now.* But that's just when you have to take a step back and look at the big picture. Honestly, sometimes it's

73

just a matter of doing it because you know that's what God has called you to do. It's about being obedient."

At the time, Riley didn't know that her willingness to fight through her selfish desires in order to serve was the first in a series of steps toward understanding the concept of worship. Just like the athletes who work on the boring fundamentals in order to improve their game and prove their love of their sport, she was worshiping God with her service.

But before she could realize that truth, Riley first had a different kind of growing to do. At birth, she was 25 inches long and jokes that she "really didn't stop growing." By the time she was 12 years old, Riley was already six feet tall. Although lanky and uncoordinated during her early teen years, she gravitated toward such sports as volleyball, track and—the most obvious choice for a Hoosier—basketball.

When Riley's athleticism finally caught up with her size, letters from NCAA Division 1 colleges started to trickle into her mailbox. After playing Amateur Athletic Union ball between her freshman and sophomore high-school years, coaching staffs really started to take notice. But the self-proclaimed homebody didn't want to go far from Macy, so Riley only took one campus visit—to Notre Dame, which is located in South Bend, Indiana.

Even though she was less than two hours from the farm in Macy, Riley's short-distance excursion was vital to her growth as a basketball player and, more importantly, as a Christian. At that point, she says her mom sat back and allowed her to choose which direction to go. Riley then "definitely chose to seek Him even more."

In 1997, Riley's freshman year, Notre Dame had a policy that did not allow ministries such as Fellowship of Christian Athletes to operate on campus. Instead, she and the other Christian athletes at Notre Dame would get together for independently led Bible studies and prayer times.

Ironically, that all changed in the fall of 2002—18 months after Riley's graduation—when first-year head football coach Tyrone Willingham (now with the University of Washington) petitioned the university to make such organizations accessible to its students. It was actually Willingham's secondary coach, Trent Walters (now with the Philadelphia Eagles), who urged the head coach to get involved.

Riley's college career met all of her expectations and then some. She was the starting center in all but seven games and became a force to reckon with on both ends of the court. Riley received First Team All-American honors as a junior and a senior, and in her final year she received the prestigious Naismith Award along with Associated Press Player of the Year honors.

However, nothing can match the feeling Riley experienced in the 2001 NCAA tournament. After making its way to the Final Four and ultimately the championship game against Purdue, Notre Dame trailed the Lady

Boilermakers 66-64 late in the second half, when Riley tied the contest with a field goal. Then, with 5.8 seconds remaining, she drew a foul and made both free throws to secure the win. Riley was also named the Final Four's Most Outstanding Player.

The next month, Riley was drafted by the WNBA's Miami Sol, where she played two seasons before the team disbanded. After spending the off-season playing in Spain, she was selected by Detroit in a dispersal draft. For the next four seasons, Riley was a key contributor to the Shock and enjoyed WNBA championship wins in 2003 and 2006. She was also named an Eastern Conference All-Star in 2005.

Riley traveled to Athens during the off-season in 2004 and helped the United States secure a gold medal at the Summer Olympics. She played two years with the Colorado Chill, a National Women's Basketball League team and was part of a championship season in 2005. Riley's hoops excursions also sent her to the Polish League prior to the 2007 WNBA season.

Riley laughs when she recalls how tentative she was about leaving home for college. Since then, she has traveled throughout the United States and has visited many foreign countries. But the most important development, Riley says, has been her rapid spiritual maturity that may not have happened otherwise.

"It wasn't until I was on my own and I got into the professional world and had to take care of myself and had the pressure of playing professional athletes," Riley says. "That's when I truly relied on my relationship with God and became more diligent in seeking Him and reading the Word and trying to understand His will for my life more."

In February 2007, Riley was traded to the San Antonio Silver Stars. Since her arrival in San Antonio, she has enjoyed the unique environment afforded by the team. "Everyone on our entire team is a Christian," Riley says. "They're not only Christians, but they desire to get together and study and pray for each other. The coaching staff is made up of all Christians as well. It's an unusual setting, but it's pretty amazing to be in the professional world where you have so many pressures and outside forces and to come in and know that you have that common bond."

As a professional athlete, Riley has been afforded numerous opportunities to get involved with various communities. In Miami—where she still resides—she has worked with the city's Rescue Mission for the homeless and low-income families. Riley has also spoken at area schools and helped build a playground in a poor neighborhood.

But in 2006, Riley stepped out in a big way when she traveled to Nairobi, Kenya, as part of a group of people hoping to get involved in finding solutions for the HIV/AIDS pandemic. After falling in love with the people, she returned to Africa two more times, with trips to Mali and South Africa. These experiences opened her eyes to the true meaning of serving.

"Serving is putting everyone before yourself," Riley says. "To me it's more about humility and a willingness to be there for others. Service doesn't have to be an organized event. It's giving of your time, which for a lot of people is the hardest thing to do. It's honestly just making yourself available and willingly giving your time to somebody else."

As part of Riley's spiritual growth process, she has learned that the act of serving others from a pure heart and out of obedience to God is truly a form of worship. She points to Luke 4, where Jesus was fasting 40 days in the wilderness while dealing with a series of temptations from Satan. After the devil offered Jesus authority over the kingdoms of the world in exchange for His worship, Jesus rebuked Satan by responding, "It is written: Worship the Lord your God, and serve Him only" (Luke 4:8).

It might not be obvious at first glance, but Riley believes that Jesus' correlation between worship and serving is quite clear. And the greater our love for God, the easier it becomes to step out and do those things that may not be fun and may not reflect our personal desires but are key to giving glory to the Father.

"If you love God, you'll obey Him," Riley says. "So your act of worship is service. If you're truly worshiping and loving and admiring who God is and what He's done in your life, it's going to be a natural process to serve. . . . My prayer is just, 'Change my heart.' I feel like your heart should be a true reflection of God and what He would want you to be doing. Just in your pure desire to follow Him, I think that service comes out of that by default—by just wanting to do what He's put before you. I just feel so blessed with what He's given me [and want to] use that in any way, whether it's talking about Him or just showing people who He is."

Just like every follower of Christ, Riley also has those moments when human nature gets in the way of serving. But that's when she says we must rely on the Holy Spirit to give us strength to push away from our selfishness and share God's message of hope and love with others through our actions and our words.

"When you don't feel like doing something, you can just pray and ask Him to create in you a heart for service," Riley says. "I think you have to be realistic that serving isn't always going to be the first thing on your list, but that's when you pray and ask God to change your heart about the situation and give you the energy to do it."

Another biblical truth that helps Riley is found in 1 Corinthians 12:4-6, where Paul writes, "Now there are different kinds of gifts, but the same Spirit. There are different ministries, but the same Lord. There are different activities, but the same God is active in everyone and everything."

"The thing I like about these verses is that God doesn't ask us to go out of our way and create a way to serve Him or serve others," Riley says. "We are just to remain available, and the opportunities come for us to use what He has already given us. Just like we don't all have the same gifts, we don't all serve the same way. There are so many ways to serve. Most of the time, God calls us to serve Him with what we are already passionate about and with the gifts that He has already given us. Don't compare yourself to others and think that we should all serve the same way."

Riley is especially attuned to the plight of athletes and coaches, whom she believes are automatically role models within their circles of influence, no matter how big or how small those circles are. That status opens up the doors for countless opportunities to serve.

"People are watching what you do," she says. "Your time and your words mean a lot to them. So the way you interact with people, you can use that as a testimony, and it's such a small thing—whether it's signing an autograph or spending time with some of your fans or just how you conduct yourself in general."

Riley has discovered that serving isn't always about massive, national campaigns or overseas ministry prospects. In fact, most of the time, it's the small things that Riley finds end up meaning so much to those who need a helping hand or an encouraging word.

"It's like sending a care package to a kid who's sick, and it changes his whole day and his week," Riley says. "It might be doing mission trips and just knowing that the small amount of time you've given does impact your life. You can make a difference. That's probably the biggest thing—knowing that spending time with people and helping them really makes a difference in the world. I think a lot of people become desensitized to so much of what's going on and think, *Why bother? It doesn't matter.* But it does matter. It matters to those people, and it matters to you. That's the beautiful thing about serving."

Another benefit of serving that Riley has grown to appreciate is the life-changing effect it has on her priorities and her perspective. Daily issues and minor inconveniences that once seemed so important pale in comparison to the plight of the poor and the hungry. Selfish ambitions that drove her to achieve greatness now hold little significance against the backdrop of entire continents suffering from deadly diseases and devastating pestilences.

For the past decade, Riley has allowed God to perform ongoing surgical procedures on her heart. In the process, she has clearly noticed a difference in her prayer life. Instead of asking what God can do for her, she now asks God what she can do for Him as a servant's act of worship.

"I look at where my life is going, and I'm just amazed at how God has used me and allowed me to share Him with others," Riley says. "Just being a vessel is humbling, and it's amazing that He allows us to do that. He allows us to be a part of who He is and what He's trying to say to this world."

TRAINING TIME

1. How much time do you spend pursuing your interests and hobbies? What ultimately drives you to give so much of yourself to those pursuits?

2. Read Luke 4:5-8. In this story, Jesus rebuked Satan's attempt to garner His worship. Why do you think Jesus responded in the way He did in verse 8? What connection can be made between worship and serving based on His words?

3. Riley says, "When you don't feel like doing something, you can just pray and ask Him to create in you a heart for serving." Describe a time when selfishness hindered your desire to serve. How did you overcome human nature in order to fulfill God's purpose?

4. Read Paul's words in 1 Corinthians 12:4-6. How might this passage open up the doors to many more opportunities to serve? In what ways do you see yourself using your unique talents, abilities and interests to serve others?

5. Read John 21:15-17. In this passage, which takes place after Jesus' resurrection, Christ tells Peter what he must do to prove his love for Him. Why do you think Jesus asked the same question three times? What does this exchange tell you about the importance of serving others in God's eyes?

"Every trip to Africa that I've been on has been an act of serving others and in some way trying to help people better their situations and to show them that somebody cares about them. When I was in Africa working with kids, it was that time of interaction—making them feel valued, making them feel like they're important—that meant the most. When we were in South Africa, part of what we were doing was to promote HIV/AIDS awareness and prevention and to teach leadership building. We taught the youth and the coaches how to be leaders in their community, how to be good role models, how to have open dialogue about HIV and AIDS. I would go out on the basketball court and spend time with the kids doing drills; and immediately the next day we could see that they were so eager to learn, and they were already implementing the things we had just taught them. There's just a hunger for somebody to come in and give them guidance. It's been amazing. A lot of people look at the problem of AIDS and Africa and it becomes overwhelming because it's so big. But you can make a huge difference in one community, and you never know what kind of impact that is going to make. . . . I didn't want to leave the state of Indiana, and here I am going to Africa and trying to use the gifts and abilities God has given me to make a difference."

—Ruth Riley

7

No Excuses

Michael Chang
Former Professional Tennis Player

Based on the gift they have received, everyone should use it to serve others, as good managers of the varied grace of God. If anyone speaks, [his speech should be] like the oracles of God; if anyone serves, [his service should be] from the strength God provides, so that in everything God may be glorified through Jesus Christ. To Him belong the glory and the power forever and ever. Amen.

1 PETER 4:10-11

Believing that I was born for the service of mankind, and regarding the care of the commonwealth as a kind of common property which like the air and the water belongs to everybody, I set myself to consider in what way mankind might be best served, and what service I was myself best fitted by nature to perform.

FRANCIS BACON

There's something about purpose, something about buying into the concept of destiny that inherently evens the odds. Nowhere will you find more examples of this principle than in the Bible, where unlikely heroes saved entire nations. Moses was a self-conscious exile with a speech problem, yet God used him to free the Israelites from Egyptian slavery. David was an undersized shepherd boy living under the shadow of his strong, able-bodied older brothers; still he was empowered to kill the mammoth Philistine warrior Goliath and rescue his people from certain defeat. Mary was a teenage girl from a nondescript lineage, but God called her to be the mother of Jesus, the Savior of the world.

Michael Chang knows a little something about purpose and destiny. The former international tennis star—often compared to David—spent 16 years on the court, slaying proverbial giants that literally stood head and shoulders above his 5' 9", 160-pound frame. He did so with the understanding that God had blessed him with quickness, accuracy and lightning-fast reflexes—the abilities necessary to be a competitive force.

Most tennis historians will likely agree that Chang's most famous match took place in the fourth round of the 1989 French Open. As the fifteenth-seeded player, the 17-year-old Chang was given little chance to pull off the upset against the number one player and three-time former French Open champion Ivan Lendl. True to expectations, Lendl won the first two sets 6-4, 6-4 and was up a break in the opening game of the third set. Chang broke Lendl's serve on the next game, however, and came back to win the set 6-3.

Even then, most believed Lendl would ultimately prevail. This was further solidified when during the fourth set, Chang began suffering from severe leg cramps. He fought valiantly, using creative tactics such as repetitive lob shots, devouring bananas and guzzling down liquids during every break in the action. Chang won the fourth set 6-3 to even the match at two sets apiece, but he quickly found himself losing 2-1 in the fifth. The cramps were especially painful when sliding hard on the red clay or charging after the ball. That's when Chang's mind gravitated toward the thought of bowing out of the match.

"I thought it wouldn't be so bad," Chang recalls. "I'd get a lot of pats on the back in the locker room; and the press would say, 'Great valiant effort, but bad luck that you lost.' And I thought, *You know, it wouldn't be such a bad thing.* I mean, I wasn't supposed to win under those circumstances anyway.

"So I actually started walking toward the chair umpire, and I got to about the service line; and the Spirit just totally convicted me. It was interesting because, the first thought that came to my mind was, *Michael, what are you doing?* And I thought to myself, *Well, I'm going to default this match.* So the Spirit convicted me by kind of saying, 'Well, Michael, you've got to understand that the winning and the losing have never been your job to take care of. The winning and losing have always been God's job to take care of. But your job has always been to go out there and compete and give 100 percent.'"

Still very unsure of his physical status and with the outcome very much in doubt, Chang walked back onto the court. It might sound cliché, but he literally began to take the game point by point, relying on an acute sense of focus and determination. If Chang had the opportunity to go for a winner, he'd hit the ball as hard as his body would allow. And one time, he even resorted to the outlandish tactic of using an underhand serve, which took Lendl by surprise and broke his concentration.

Then the unexpected happened. The momentum began to swing in Chang's direction. He started winning points, and those points turned into games; and before he knew it, he had won the fifth set (6-3) and the match (3-2). To this day, Chang occasionally goes back and watches video of the contest and admittedly "can't understand or comprehend how that match was won." He has, however, been able to decipher multiple purposes achieved as a result of the victory, one of which was the uplifting of an entire culture—the Chinese people.

"The match with Lendl is evidence of what God can do and [evidence of] His power," Chang says. "Certainly, being 17, I was not expected to win; and I wasn't expected to come back from two sets to love down against Lendl. But God has His funny ways of showing His power, and He has His funny ways of allowing the weak things of the world to shame the strong and allowing the ordinary things of the world to become extraordinary. That match was one of those times."

Chang went on to defeat Stefan Edberg in the finals to become the youngest winner of a Grand Slam tournament. More importantly, he learned a number of lessons. First and foremost, he learned to never give up. He says that truth has stayed with him for years. His French Open experience often reminds him to stick with it when difficult circumstances abound. But another piece of Chang's education during those two weeks in Paris came from the realization that the words written in Romans 8:28 are absolutely true: "We know that all things work together for the good of those who love God; those who are called according to His purpose."

"I certainly walked away with a better appreciation for how God made me in stature or being Chinese," Chang says. "I used to question that when I was younger. But I realize now that both of those things were all to give God greater glory. I think if I was 6'2" or 6'3" and could overpower everybody, then it would be much easier for people to say, 'Well, Michael did it in his own strength.' But instead there's no question about why things happened the way they happened."

Chang has never been one to make excuses for why or how things happen. This invaluable principle was imparted into his life at a very young age. He was born in Hoboken, New Jersey, to Chinese immigrants who met in the United States. Joe Chang was born in Taiwan and came to America for graduate school. Betty Chang was born in New Delhi, India. Her father was a Chinese diplomat to the Dominican Republic. Her being born in India was a result of her parents' frequent international travel. Like Joe, Betty's family ultimately migrated to the United States as a matter of protection from political, civil and social unrest in their homeland.

Chang's parents settled into new jobs and started a family. By the time he was seven years old, Chang was playing tennis along with his brother, Carl. The siblings had grown up watching his mom and dad play recreationally. Joe Chang, in fact, played in several company tournaments.

As Chang developed his game, he began playing in public events around town. That led to entries in some junior tournaments and eventually the national amateur circuit. At the age of 12, he claimed the United States Tennis Association Junior Hard Court singles title. A year later, he claimed the Fiesta Bowl 16s bracket championship. In 1987, a 15-year old Chang won the USTA Boys 18s Hardcourt event and the Boys 18s National title. He also became the youngest player to win a main draw match at the U.S. Open by defeating Paul McNamee in the first round.

Before then, Chang had never considered turning professional. If anything, his parents thought their sons might be good enough to secure tennis scholarships for college. But now, he was on the road to a full-blown career in tennis. Strangely, Chang was unlike many of the day's young stars who came from affluent backgrounds and were practically bred to succeed in the sport.

Instead, his family charted a more difficult path. His mother quit her job and followed him for the first four years of his career. Eventually, Carl—who played doubles with Chang early on—would set aside his personal aspirations and serve as his brother's coach. Those sacrifices have given the International Tennis Hall of Fame inductee a greater appreciation for all of his achievements.

"I think that everybody has to go through a learning process," Chang says. "I'm certainly no different than that. But I think the difference for me was the things that I learned through the Bible and through being in church and from those people around me who are in leadership roles. My mom and dad are probably two of the best examples of that. Growing up, neither of my parents came from wealthy families. They were very much middle-class families, and they didn't have a honeymoon until their twenty-fifth wedding anniversary. All of their extra money would also be put toward my brother and me for tennis lessons or gifts that we wanted and different things like that. My parents sacrificed everything they had for us."

It didn't take long for Chang to realize that his small stature wasn't the only thing that made him stand out on tour. He was one of the few Christians in the game. In fact, Chang says he can count on one hand how many believers he came across in 16 years as a professional. Although he never felt persecuted or rejected—most of his peers actually respected him for his beliefs—he certainly had moments when being an outspoken defender of the faith put him at a disadvantage. His experience at the 1989 French Open was particularly difficult.

"After the match [against Lendl] was over, people asked, 'Michael, why did you win today?'" Chang remembers. "And I said, 'Well, I won because of the Lord Jesus Christ.' The following day, the press that I got was unbelievably negative. My next three matches were played under conditions that I've never experienced in my career. I've never had crowds literally boo me. When I walked onto the court and warmed up, they weren't just rooting for my opponent, they were actually rooting against me. It was a really strange feeling."

Fortunately, Chang wasn't alone. While he had no one to lean on in the locker room, his family did provide the spiritual support he needed to press forward. Throughout his career, he always had at least one member of his family traveling with him.

"That provided a great deal of fellowship and also an opportunity to pray together, to learn together and to grow together," Chang says. "I didn't get a chance to go to church as much as I would have liked, but I feel that God understood my situation. My Sundays were usually spent playing in a final or traveling to my next destination. But through listening to sermons and listening to music and fellowshipping with whoever was with me, God really taught us a great deal as a family about Him and who He is and what our purpose was out there on the tennis court."

Supported by his family, Chang strung together one of the most decorated careers for any American player. He won 34 singles titles and finished second in 24 tournaments. Chang was a member of the 1990 U.S. Davis Cup championship team, and he helped lead the 1993 U.S. World Team Cup squad to victory. He was ranked as high as number two in the world during the 1996 season; and by the time he retired in 2003, he had more than $19 million in prize earnings.

Aside from racking up impressive finishes and earnings during his career, Chang was also known as one of the most active players in the realm of community service and humanitarian-related causes. In fact, in 1999, Chang established the Chang Family Foundation as part of an effort to reach people for Jesus through local community and international programs.

In 2002, the foundation launched the Christian Sports League, which partners with local churches and ministries as a way to share the gospel through organized and competitive sports. The league is currently operational in Seattle, Washington, and Orange County, California, with plans to open branches throughout the western United States and beyond.

Just as it was during his career, Chang continues to have a "no excuses" mentality in life. This is particularly true when it comes to serving. In this realm, Chang's efforts have only increased since leaving the game, and the topic is one for which he has an overwhelming passion. One thing that Chang has observed is that many people use fear and uncertainty as an excuse for not helping others. He says this is a natural emotion but can be dealt with much easier after asking oneself some tough questions.

"Sometimes people are uncomfortable when they get outside of their comfort zone, and they don't know how God is going to use them," Chang says. "But the question isn't how God is going to use you. The question is really, Are you going to have an open heart to serve and to be stretched? That's the real question. It's not, Am I old enough? Am I talented enough? Am I smart enough? Do I know the Bible well enough? It has nothing to do with these things. The question is, Are you ready to be used by God?"

But Chang contends that sometimes it just boils down to pride. This is especially true for those who are in positions of prominence or those who come from wealthy families where entitlement may be part of the equation. "The world's natural inclination for people in those situations is for them to want people to serve them," Chang says. "But if you're in a situation where you're able to encourage people, to support people, to go out of your way to help people and serve them in various ways, it makes you stand out. People are going to wonder why you do things the way that you do. For me, the biggest reason is because my Lord and Savior is that way, and I try to be like Jesus."

93

TRAINING TIME

1. Michael Chang is often compared to the biblical hero David. Who are some other people (from the Bible, from history or from modern day society) who have overcome immense odds to do great things? What character traits do you think those people might have in common?

2. Read Romans 8:28. Can you describe a time when you questioned God about certain aspects of your existence? How might this Scripture give you a peace about such concerns?

3. Read 1 Peter 4:10-11. What are some talents and abilities with which God has blessed you? How does this Scripture challenge you to use those to serve others? Peter tells us that our service should be "from the strength God provides." How might that admonition make the challenge of serving easier to face?

4. What are some excuses you give when it comes to serving? What are some ways you can move past the excuses into an attitude of humility and service?

5. Chang says, "When God sees where your heart is and you're doing His work, He always provides." How does the promise of provision empower you to serve regardless of the circumstances?

"There's a lady named Kay Abe. She's been serving the homeless in downtown Seattle for over 30 years. I remember one time when I was serving there and feeding the homeless. I was the one distributing the rice. So there were maybe about 150, 200 people in line. I'm putting the rice on the people's plates, and I'm looking at how much rice we have left. I look at the line, and I say to the person next to me, 'There's not enough rice.' I eat rice almost every day, and I know when there's not enough rice. I'm thinking that this might be the only good meal these homeless people will have for quite some time. So I said to Kay, 'What are we going to do?' and she said, 'Don't worry about it. Just keep giving it the way you've been giving it.' So I keep serving it until I get to the last person, and there's just enough rice. I was just so shocked. So I asked Kay, 'I know that there wasn't enough rice. You know that there wasn't enough rice. Why is it that you have the faith to tell me not to worry about it?' And she said, 'I've seen it time and time again. When God sees where your heart is and you're doing His work, He always provides.' That's where your faith and your story come from. That's where you get excited about doing God's work, because incredible things like that happen."

—Michael Chang

8

BALANCING ACT

Jarome Iginla
NHL Right Wing

I have become all things to all men so that by all possible means
I might save some. I do all this for the sake of the gospel,
that I may share in its blessings.

1 CORINTHIANS 9:22-23, *NIV*

Do all the good you can, by all the means you can,
in all the ways you can, in all the places you can,
at all the times you can, to all the people you can,
as long as ever you can.

JOHN WESLEY

When sports fans think about hockey—and in particular the NHL—there's no telling what imagery might come to mind. For some, hockey is all about the pinpoint passing skills. For others, it's the forceful nature of the slap shot. Some might even reference the catlike prowess of the ever-alert goalkeepers, and their distinctive protective gear and colorful masks. Of course, most can't talk about hockey without mentioning the bone-crushing cross-checks into the boards or those legendary (if not mandatory) nightly brawls.

But one of the game's most overlooked fundamentals is the irreplaceable discipline of balance. Burly men in bulky pads fly around on razor-thin blades while changing directions every few seconds. The same is true for the goalies, who must remain steady in precarious crouching positions as would-be scorers approach the net.

As an elite professional hockey player, Jarome Iginla knows a little something about balance. Since debuting in the NHL during the 1996-97 season, the Calgary Flames' right wing has appeared in four All-Star Games and been among the league's leaders in points and goals. Iginla has used the concept of balance to employ both power and finesse in his game, depending on what the given situation might require. He is also known for having one of the most powerful slap shots in the NHL.

Still, no matter how many accolades Iginla receives, he is just as known for being one of a select few black players in the NHL and perhaps one of the most-decorated black athletes to ever take the ice. In 2007-08, the league's 30 teams only touted a total of 16 black players. Even though Willie O'Ree broke the color barrier in 1958 when he joined the Boston Bruins, diversity in the league has been a slow process.

Iginla doesn't bemoan that harsh reality. After all, it's something he grew up with as the biracial son of a Nigerian father and a white mother from Oregon. That made life interesting for a kid growing up in Edmonton, Alberta, who fell in love with the sport of hockey.

"When I grew up, I was the only black kid on my team," Iginla says. "I was aware of that. I really was. I was very fortunate. My teammates were always great. But sometimes there'd be a small incident here or there with another team or with some parents in the crowd. Some kids would say, 'Why are you trying to be in the NHL? There's no black players in the NHL.' I remember those questions back then and honestly, it meant so much to me to be able to say, 'Oh yeah, there are black players in the NHL.' Grant Fuhr at the time was starring in Edmonton and winning Stanley Cups, and he was an All-Star. I tried to pick out as many black players in the NHL, so I could have somebody. I watched guys like Claude Vilgrain and Tony McKegney."

Iginla used that inspiration to climb the junior hockey ranks all the way to the top. In October 2003, he made history when he was named captain of the Flames. With that honor, Iginla became just the second black captain in the NHL (Dirk Graham of the Chicago Blackhawks was the first). In 2001-02, Iginla also became the first black player to win the regular season point and goal scoring titles.

"I am proud to be a black player in the NHL," he says. "I know how much those other guys meant to me, so maybe there's kids that are having similar questions asked of them or maybe they're having some tough times. It would be an honor if I was at all a role model for black kids that want to play in the NHL."

Iginla also learned the art of balance from his unique experiences at home. His parents—Elvis Iginla and Susan

Schuchard—separated when he was a baby and eventually divorced. His father was going to law school, so his mother raised him with the help of his maternal grandparents. It was their gift of serving that made a lasting impression on Iginla that still resonates today.

"My grandparents are extremely generous people," he says. "They had eight kids and they had tons of grandkids. They had already done their parenting, and still they took me to practices after school when my mom couldn't because she was working. They got me involved in as many activities as they could. I always went to their house after school, and I always felt loved. I never felt like a burden. When I look back on it, I realize that they were second parents to me, and that was very generous of them. They were huge examples in my life."

When it came to matters of faith, however, Iginla points to his father as the most important influence. Ironically, his mother was a Buddhist but never pushed her religious beliefs on her son. It certainly made for some interesting conversations growing up, but when it came time for Iginla to make his own decision about faith, his choice was ultimately spurred by a late-night conversation that took place on a trip with his junior hockey team. Iginla was 14 at the time, and his friend started a conversation about the existence of God by asking, "What if there's no God?" Iginla, who attended Catholic school, insisted that there had to be a God. It was something he had always believed to be true, but the thought that God might not exist was troubling.

"He got me thinking, and it actually scared me for a little bit," Iginla says. "I'd never really thought about it that deep. It was just from what I'd read. I'd never thought about it personally. So that bothered me, and I tried not to think about that for a while."

About a year later, he approached his father about the subject. Elvis Iginla, who grew up a Muslim before converting to Christianity, suggested that his son pray and ask God to take that fear away. If he felt a peace, then he would know that God existed.

"That's probably my defining moment," Iginla says. "It was. I'm peaceful with that now. That was probably the most bothersome question that I can ever remember asking myself. When my dad told me that, it was probably the start of my own personal relationship [with Christ]."

When Iginla turned 16, he moved to British Columbia, where he played junior hockey for three years. He was then drafted by the Dallas Stars in 1995 but traded to Calgary, where he has played his entire career. Along the way, Iginla has also enjoyed great success as a member of the Canadian national men's team. He played in two Olympics (2002 and 2006), one World Championship (1997), one World Junior Championship (1996) and one World Cup of Hockey (2004). All told, Iginla has won four international gold medals, but none was more special than the 2002 victory in Salt Lake City.

"That's one of the best experiences I had in hockey," Iginla says. "I got a chance to play with Mario Lemieux and Steve Yzerman and Joe Sakic. It's a big adjustment. You go from playing against them to seeing your jersey hanging in the same room as theirs. It was difficult not to be in awe. Then we ended up winning the tournament. I remember the first day showing up and seeing all those jerseys hanging and seeing mine over in the corner. I was one of the younger guys, and I had a makeshift area, because there weren't enough lockers. But it was a huge thrill, and I think I probably took a picture or something."

The 2002 gold-medal contest was against the host U.S. team and is considered by many hockey historians to be one of the most electrically charged atmospheres the international game has ever experienced. Iginla, no doubt, concurs with that analysis.

"It was probably the most exciting game I've been a part of," he says. "It was so fast. The fans were so passionate. Half of them were American fans, and the other half were Canadians. They were going at it the whole game. It was such a good game. You get on the ice and go as hard as you can. You don't have time to be nervous. You get off the ice, and you're nervous again, because you're watching as a fan. You want to win the gold medal so bad. It turned out the way we wanted it to turn out. It was every emotion—nervousness, excitement, adrenaline—all in one game."

As a star NHL player and a key national team figure, Iginla has been afforded certain luxuries that come with money and notoriety. So often, athletes that come from humble beginnings struggle to balance their new lifestyle with the people they used to be—but not Iginla. Thanks to the strong foundation laid down by his family years earlier, he has resisted the temptation to be proud and demanding and instead chooses to serve others the way his grandparents served him.

"In being a Christian and serving God, I think it's trying to be a positive influence in the lives of people you come into contact with and your friends and your family," Iginla says. "With all the gifts that have been given to us, we should make the most of them. Some people are more outspoken, and some people glorify God in different ways. So I think everyone has been given unique gifts, and we all play a different role."

When Iginla first joined the Flames, he admits that there weren't many personal requests to speak or make appearances for various organizations around Calgary. But that all changed as he emerged as one of the team's veteran leaders and one of the league's more popular players. Iginla says he isn't doing any less but unfortunately feels like he's saying no more often. In searching for that balance, Iginla has received some life-changing revelations.

"Just reading the Bible has helped," Iginla says. "I've learned that serving is about your family and friends and your everyday life. I don't believe serving is just about getting involved out in the community. I do think it starts at home and being a positive influence on your kids and being grateful and being thankful. It starts inward and comes out."

Iginla also cites as revelatory a television sermon he once heard that was based on the popular phrase, "What Would Jesus Do?" The preacher talked about how serving isn't always about doing more but making sure there's a qualitative measure in the serving that ultimately involves keeping one's priorities in order.

"You might have to get some rest or take some family time," Iginla says. "Serving is also about your family and making sure you're there for them and trying to be a role model for your kids and making sure their needs are taken care of and your wife's needs are taken care of. It is a balance. But I think, even in the home stuff, you're still serving. There are different ways to serve; and it's not always charities—which are great and everything—but I do believe there are a number of different ways to serve, and when it might not look like you're serving, you probably still are."

Iginla's strong commitment to wife, Kara, daughter, Jade, and son, Tij, however, does not preclude him from doing his part to serve as an ambassador of his team, of his league and, most importantly, of his faith. His first act of service is to be a positive influence, although the rigors of the job sometimes present challenges in that area.

"I know I'm not always [a positive influence]," Iginla candidly admits. "I know I have bad days and grumpy days. I try to limit those. But I try to take time to sign some extra autographs. I know that's not a big deal, but for young kids or people who are big hockey fans, it might just put a smile on their face. From the small things to the big things, that's the goal, and I think that goes back to my definition of serving. It's a lot of small things. It's not always about a big charity but having that little extra moment to ask kids how they're doing. I think Jesus would want us to do our best in the small things or in the big things. I totally believe it's not just about meeting people's physical needs. It's also about meeting their emotional needs."

On a larger scale, Iginla has certainly done his fair share of serving throughout Calgary and its surrounding areas. He supports Cure for Cancer, and he and his wife organize a nonprofit hockey school every summer, with the proceeds going to charity. In 2004, he received the NHL Foundation Award for Community Service and the King Clancy Memorial Trophy, both of which recognize outstanding humanitarian contributions.

One of Iginla's favorite serving opportunities comes through his participation in the efforts of a Calgary-based program called KidSport, which helps kids overcome financial obstacles that prevent their participation in sports. "Families can turn to it for help," he says. "It means a lot to me. I think all kids should have an opportunity to play—and not just to become a professional athlete but to enjoy themselves and make friends and learn life skills. I was very fortunate to have the support that I did, and not every kid does."

"I'm extremely blessed in so many ways," he adds. "I want to serve Christ, and in doing that I want to give back in as many different ways and positive ways as I can. By serving my family and friends and others, I'm trying to say thank You to God. That's what I'm trying to do every day."

Iginla is convinced that a lifestyle of serving should reflect the same kind of diversity that he inherently adds as a prominent black player in the NHL. Serving can and should appear in diverse guises, as evidenced in 1 Corinthians 12:27-28, which lists the different important roles believers play in the Body of Christ: apostles, prophets, teachers, miracle workers, healers, helpers, administrators, and those speaking in different kinds of tongues.

"Some people are more evangelical, and I think there are all different types of Christians," Iginla says. "By types, I mean we have different roles in serving God and getting His message out. Some are more outspoken and some are less outspoken. Some do it more quietly. Some do it through generosity of time or money. And when I talked to my dad growing up, that was part of me working on getting more comfortable with things and trying to know where I fit.

"I'm not as outspoken as some people and maybe more so than others," he concludes. "But we all have a purpose in serving."

TRAINING TIME

1. What are some of life's daily challenges that hinder you from serving? Have you been able to overcome those challenges? If so, how?

2. Read 1 Corinthians 9:22. What do you think Paul means when he says he becomes "all things to all men"? In what ways can you be more flexible in your approach to serving?

3. Throughout the Bible, people such as Moses, David and even Jesus took time to rest. Can you describe a time when you felt the need to break from your normal routine in athletics, work or ministry? How does that time away from consistent serving help refresh and energize you?

4. Read Isaiah 40:31. What are some of the promises found in this passage? How can trusting in or waiting on the Lord impact your desire to serve others?

5. Iginla says, "We have different roles in serving God and getting His message out." Read 1 Corinthians 12:27-29. Take the ministries listed in those Scriptures and think of some opportunities to serve that best fit the gifts, talents, personality traits and interests God has placed in you. How does knowing there are many ways to serve take away some of the pressure to conform to other people's concept of serving?

"My father has always been a real strong influence on my faith and questions that I had. He was someone I leaned on. It's hard to talk about serving and some of the things that we do, because growing up, I learned from him that you don't necessarily want to draw attention to yourself for doing it. But I would see different things. People would come to him on the street, needing money, even if it was just a couple of dollars. He wouldn't just give it to them, but he'd talk to them and ask them what their situation was. Those types of things had an influence on me as far as giving and serving. As a young kid, I always wondered why those people weren't working, and he would always say, 'We don't know their story.' It might not make a difference, and there's always a debate whether or not you should help, but that's the way he felt. Sometimes he would give them 20 dollars if he felt like they were really needy, or he would give them two dollars. It was just however he felt God was directing him. Those are just things that happened when I was maybe 10 years old, and it helped guide me. He definitely told me why he did these things. He sat me down if I had questions and would answer them. He tried to give me a better understanding. He was my dad, but he was also my role model."

—Jarome Iginla

9

LIKE A GOOD NEIGHBOR

Danny Wuerffel
Former NCAA and NFL Quarterback

Love the Lord your God with all your heart, with all your soul, with all your mind, and with all your strength. The second is: Love your neighbor as yourself. There is no other commandment greater than these.

MARK 12:30-31

Wherever a man turns he can find someone who needs him.

ALBERT SCHWEITZER

As the son of an Air Force chaplain, Danny Wuerffel had lots of neighbors growing up. He had neighbors in South Carolina, Nebraska, Colorado and even Spain. Eventually Wuerffel's family settled in Fort Walton Beach, Florida, where he developed into one of the state's outstanding quarterbacks. And while most kids in his shoes might have fallen prey to becoming typical military brats, Wuerffel had a much different understanding of his circumstances.

"The Scriptures say to love the Lord your God with all of your heart, mind, soul and strength and to love your neighbor as yourself," Wuerffel says. "But we are unfortunately caught up with focusing most of our passions not on loving our neighbor but loving and caring and serving ourselves."

Wuerffel's well-balanced attitude—grounded by his strong Christian upbringing—was not only fortified by the example set by his father's military service but was equally modeled by his mother, Lola, a stay-at-home mom with a big heart.

"My mother was probably the first person to really model serving to me," Wuerffel says. "She was a phenomenal mother, caring for all the needs of her children; and as I grew up, I learned she was a very talented musician growing up and had different opportunities to pursue that. It was a deep love and passion for her, but as she became a wife and mother, she chose to serve her husband and to serve her children above her own interests. She cultivated a heart that loved and enjoyed doing that. So she was and continues to be one of the greatest servants that I know."

But as a teenager, Wuerffel admits that his idea of being a Christian was mostly about being good and avoiding bad behavior. In high school, this attitude (albeit misguided) certainly had its merits. The young football star stayed out of trouble and performed exceptionally in the classroom. In fact, Wuerffel graduated as the class valedictorian. His playing career was pretty phenomenal as well, made evident by his team's 4A state title in 1991 and number two national ranking in *USA Today* that same year.

Wuerffel's stellar high-school career led to a scholarship offer from the University of Florida, where he led the Gators to four Southeastern Conference titles from 1993 to 1996 and the National Championship in 1996. He was also the 1996 Heisman Trophy winner and ended his college career with a combined 17 NCAA and Florida records.

Amid the staggering hype, the two-time All-American and two-time Davey O'Brien Award winner took the first step in a painstaking process of discovering the true nature of having a personal relationship with Christ. While many of Wuerffel's teammates were taking full advantage of their newfound freedoms in college, he found himself studying the Bible with an older gentleman who became Wuerffel's most-trusted mentor.

"We began studying in the Scriptures, and I was overcome by God's holiness," Wuerffel says. "To see how holy God was began to expose more and more the parts of my heart that I grew to realize weren't holy. Sin was not only the things that I did, but things that I said, things that I was thinking and the motives for the things that I did. So I realized that many of the things that motivated me to be a good person were fear, worrying about what people think, image and reputation, and that even the good things I did were so often motivated by sinful things. That really put me back on my knees, craving forgiveness."

As he grew closer to God, Wuerffel also discovered the importance of being involved with a community of believers. That led him to the University of Florida's Fellowship of Christian Athletes chapter, where he became a dedicated member and faithful participant. Wuerffel is still actively involved with FCA and regularly speaks at the University of Florida as well as at other FCA venues throughout the region.

When Wuerffel was drafted by the New Orleans Saints in 1997, he took his burgeoning desire to serve others with him. It didn't take long for Wuerffel to hear about a local ministry that was founded seven years earlier by a man named Mo Leverett. His program—Desire Street Ministries—was located in the Ninth Ward's infamous Desire Street neighborhood, which was historically known as the city's worst neighborhood due to the prevalence of drugs, violence and depravity. Initially, Wuerffel had no plans to get involved. That all changed after he made that first visit.

"As I drove in, I saw this old housing project created in the 1950s," Wuerffel says. "At one point it had over 15,000 people living in a small area, stacked on top of each other with a barbed-wire fence around. It was said to keep them safe but looked more like a prison than a community. It was known as one of the most dangerous places in the country to live, with the highest crime rate. As I drove in the project, the buildings were in such bad condition that they looked like they should have been condemned years before. Not only were they not condemned, they were still standing. I thought it had to be a danger to live there; and as I was considering the terrible state of these buildings, a little girl walked out of one of the buildings with a doll. I realized she lived in that building. It just didn't make sense.

"It made me frustrated, sad and confused. Here I was playing professional football a few miles from this place in the Superdome—the Superdome where we played the Sugar Bowl and the National Championship for the University of Florida—and yet in this place not far from me, it looked more like a third-world country than what you would expect in a city of the United States of America."

Once Wuerffel got involved with Desire Street Ministries, he was immediately hooked. He started volunteering, teaching Bible studies, playing with the kids and helping to raise money. Through his efforts, many new facilities were built, including a gymnasium, a health clinic and a school. Even though he was still playing in the NFL, Wuerffel was giving equal amounts of time and energy to Desire Street.

"One of the first things that attracted me to the ministry was looking in the eyes of these children and seeing so much God-given potential," Wuerffel says. "But this situation they were born into created so few opportunities for them to fulfill their God-given potential and use their gifts. So the children drew me in."

During that time, Wuerffel continued to play in the NFL, although his professional career paled in comparison to the success he had experienced at the collegiate level. Over the next seven years, he spent time with the Saints, the Green Bay Packers, the Chicago Bears and the

Washington Redskins. Wuerffel even spent time as a member of the Rhein Fire in the now-defunct NFL Europe, where he was named MVP of the World Bowl in 2000.

By January 2004, Wuerffel was unsigned but still planning to continue his career. He decided to work part-time with Desire Street Ministries while spending the rest of his day training and seeking out a free-agency deal. But by February, Wuerffel found himself terribly conflicted and felt torn between his two very different worlds.

"Every day I was driving down Canal Boulevard to get on the interstate, and every time I would have to turn right to go train and continue my dream of playing with the NFL," Wuerffel remembers. "So I would have to turn right to go practice football, but I would have to turn left to go to Desire Street; and every day it got harder and harder to turn right. After a little bit of time of doing that, I ended up retiring from the NFL and went to work full time with Desire Street Ministries."

Finally, the call to serve won out, and Wuerffel retired from professional football in order to pursue full-time ministry—a lifestyle that the athletic man describes as "incredibly exhausting and exhilarating." Desire Street Ministries was extremely successful in transforming the lives of kids who were previously selling drugs, carrying guns and stealing cars. Their lives were being changed by God's love and the teaching of the gospel. Wuerffel says many of these young people are now married and raising children, having broken the vicious cycle of hopelessness.

And then there was Katrina. It was August 2005 when the iconic hurricane swept across the Gulf Coast, leaving a path of horrific destruction that devastated significant portions of Louisiana, Mississippi, Alabama and the Florida panhandle. The Ninth Ward was particularly challenged by hurricane damage, and Desire Street Ministries faced some difficult decisions.

"If I even tried to recall all the things that really made it look impossible to continue, we would be here forever," Wuerffel says. "The ministry was completely flooded and devastated. Everybody was spread all over the country. There was no way to communicate. We were afraid thousands had died. The staff was charged to take care of the students that were scattered and lost. They, including my family, had lost all of their possessions. We all had our own personal crises to deal with in the midst of the devastation with children and the families. And to make matters worse, it was at a time at the end of the summer when funds were really low, and we didn't know if we could continue. Yet one by one, God just walked us through, around and above each of these challenges and insurmountable obstacles."

Slowly but surely, Wuerffel and the rest of the Desire Street team began picking up the pieces. Initially, the ministry was reestablished in Florida. Wuerffel found people to help him find the students from Desire Street Academy—the educational arm of Desire Street Ministries—and bring them from shelters back to the new home base.

Eventually, the school was moved to Baton Rouge, Louisiana, in time for the 2006-07 academic year. Many of its students are male high-school students who were displaced from New Orleans, but youth from Baton Rouge are also finding their way to the ministry.

The two-year process was exhausting on all levels, but Wuerffel believes that both his family and the ministry are stronger for having pushed through the trials. "I was drained in ways I never thought I could be, but at the same time my spirit was so alive," he says. "And spiritually I never felt closer to the Lord. I was so dependent on Him in intense personal moments of worship. So I just praised God in the midst of the most difficult times in which He was working, leading and guiding us. He was replenishing our hearts and our souls."

One of the most amazing aspects of Wuerffel's story is the fact that he walked away from what could have been a much longer NFL career in order to pursue a life of serving. It was a bold leap of faith that is virtually unheard of in today's self-absorbed, materialistic culture.

"It seems I have continued to get a lot of the attention in terms of the sacrifice that I've made," Wuerffel says. "I guess in some ways it was a sacrifice—certainly in terms of making a lot of money. I think there were a lot more things that would be considerably easier to do that would be a lot less stressful for me and my family. But at the same time, I really don't feel like it has been a sacrifice. I feel like it was the natural thing for me to do. When I finally discussed retiring from the NFL with my wife, because I felt the Lord was leading me to go full time with the ministry, I thought she would be surprised. But her reaction was very telling. She said very calmly that she thought this is what I would be doing all along, because that is what I liked to do."

Wuerffel is also quick to point out others in the ministry who "have made considerably more sacrifices." He is very thankful to be part of a team that includes so many faithful servants. But when it comes to personal sacrifice, Wuerffel is much more interested in what the Bible has to say. In 2 Corinthians 4:18, for example, the apostle Paul wrote, "So we do not focus on what is seen, but on what is unseen; for what is seen is temporary, but what is unseen is eternal."

It's that spiritual reality that inspires Wuerffel to look at God's big picture and spend less time worrying about temporal things such as professional ambitions, materialistic gains, personal grievances and physical vanities. For Wuerffel, that means opening his eyes and noticing what is going on in the world around him.

"One of the biggest problems in America is that we are so busy," Wuerffel says. "We can live for days and weeks, even years, in a very small bubble. We get up and go to work, we come home, we go in the garage and shut the door. We don't even know our neighbors. We may have a small group of people we associate with, but we insulate ourselves from the devastation we might see on the news, to the reality of suffering that is all around us. So as we open our eyes to see—and we don't have to see far—but if we take the effort to look around us and take the energy to look around and see people that are broken and people that are suffering, it can be discouraging. I think that it's one of the reasons we hide from it. That is why the verse 2 Corinthians 4:18 is so powerful. It gives us power to see those things—not to just see them for what they are, but to see them from an eternal perspective."

Along with the newly reestablished Desire Street Academy in Baton Rouge, Wuerffel is working toward going back to New Orleans and redeveloping the ministry in its original home. Desire Street Ministries is also supporting programs similar to its own, including an outreach program in the west side of Montgomery, Alabama, which is being patterned after Desire Street.

And for Wuerffel, all of those endeavors simply represent the beginning of a life-long commitment to fulfill the second great commandment found in Mark 12:31. In that powerful passage, Jesus flatly tells all of His followers, "Love your neighbor as yourself."

"While I look at someone that is hurting, as I look at a broken community," Wuerffel says, "I pray that God would give me the ability and honesty to look and understand it. I pray that I have the ability to fix my eyes on eternity and see what God can do in the midst of this brokenness. The things I see are temporary, and what God is doing is eternal, and that gives me great hope and confidence that my serving is not in vain."

TRAINING TIME

1. In college, Danny Wuerffel discovered that "sin was not only the things that I did, but things that I said, things that I was thinking and the motives for the things that I did." How does his realization line up with your concept of living the Christian life?

2. What motivates you to do your best in athletics, in school or on the job? How much of your desires are driven by what other people think about you versus what God thinks about you? What would you say motivates you to serve others?

3. Read James 1:27. When you read this verse, do you feel indifferent, inspired, overwhelmed or something else? What are some practical ways you might start to live out the command to take care of orphans, widows and people who are less fortunate than you?

4. Read 2 Corinthians 4:18. What usually comes to mind when you are considering the concept of eternity? How might thinking more often about eternity change the way you approach serving?

5. Read Mark 12:28-31. Who do you think Jesus is referring to when He talks about neighbors? How does the command to love your neighbor as yourself affect the way you look at those around you? How does it change your current desire to serve and bless others?

"I know in life, a lot of times people feel a tug on their heart to give of themselves to serve. I think there are so many reasons why we don't take that step, and I really think the bottom line is fear. But as we begin to trust God and see God, we begin to lay our fears before Him. He begins to show us the freedom to go beyond our fear and to serve. I think another reason people don't serve is because they are trying to identify what to do and what makes sense. If I serve, does that mean I have to go to China and be a missionary? I think with a little bit of guidance and understanding, people would realize what serving is. It is taking your natural God-given abilities and applying them to the Kingdom. He wouldn't want us to continue to do things that aren't using our talents or that would be burying our talents and not using them to glorify God. If we do what we are good at, we can serve the Kingdom. We can serve in the way that He's called us. It might be cooking or cleaning or serving in business administration or finance. There are so many ways to serve and to find where your gifts meet a need. One of the key steps is to start seeking and looking for our place and trusting that God will lead us there."

—Danny Wuerffel

Open Hearts

Betsy King
Former LPGA Golfer

By this all people will know that you are My disciples,
if you have love for one another.

JOHN 13:35

It is not how much we do, but how much love we put in the doing.
It is not how much we give, but how much love we put in the giving.

MOTHER TERESA

For nearly 30 years, Betsy King spent the majority of her time on the golf course. In most people's opinion—whether sports analysts or average fans—she did some pretty significant things in a career that resulted in 34 LPGA Tour event titles, 6 major championships, and inductions into the World Golf Hall of Fame (1995) and the LPGA Hall of Fame (2000).

Yet while King was racking up every accolade available within the realm of professional women's golf, a nagging doubt lingered about the importance of her role as an athlete and what life after sports might look like. Those thoughts were intensified after she read the book *Half Time: Changing Your Game Plan from Success to Significance* by Bob Buford.

"The book is about how you spend the first half of your life building your security and then you spend the second half of your life doing something significant," King says. "When I was playing on the tour, I always wondered what I was going to do next. I didn't know what God wanted me to do after the tour. I had a hard time thinking about that."

Questions about a future away from golf were the furthest things from King's mind as a teenage girl growing up in the mid-sized town of Redding, Pennsylvania, about an hour's drive northwest of Philadelphia. The daughter of a physician, she was eight years old when she started playing the game at a country club where her parents were members. As King entered high school, she also developed an interest in field hockey, softball and basketball. She took her love of sports to Furman University in South Carolina, where she was a three-sport athlete. As a senior, she focused solely on golf, which propelled her to the professional ranks.

Previous to her time on the LPGA Tour, King was raised in a stereotypical religious home. She attended church every week and went to Sunday School. But King realized later in life that something was missing.

"We went to a mainline church where they didn't really talk about a personal relationship with Christ," King says. "Even though I learned some of the Bible stories, it was about more than knowing the stories, and I don't think I really understood. Yeah, I knew that Jesus died for the sin of the world, but I didn't personalize the fact that Jesus died for my sin."

King's spiritual paradigm slowly began to shift in December 1979 when Bill Lewis—founder of the FCA Golf Ministry—invited her to an FCA Pro-Am fund-raising event. Lewis was also from Redding and organized player-led Bible studies. He also had a book ministry that gave the golfers access to a wide array of Christian books and Bibles. A month later, King (who had been on the tour since 1977) attended a retreat for LPGA golfers called Tee Off, and it was there that she experienced God in a brand-new way.

"I didn't make a profession of faith or commit my life to Christ until January 1980," King says. "Bruce Wilkinson was the speaker at the LPGA Fellowship retreat. There were maybe 30 of us there and he gave the chance to accept Christ after one of his talks."

Wilkinson, founder of the popular Walk Through the Bible Ministries, would go on to write the bestselling book *The Prayer of Jabez*. King would move on to achieve greatness on the LPGA Tour. She won the U.S. Open in 1989 and 1990 and claimed the LPGA Championship in 1992. King also won the Women's British Open in 1985, which at the time had yet to be declared a major.

King was also a stalwart of the United States Solheim Cup team, which competes biennially against the best golfers from Europe. She helped her team to victories in 1990, 1994, 1996 and 1998 and was part of the runner-up team in 1992. King was also honored to serve as the team captain in 2007 when the U.S. team defeated the Europeans 16-12 in Halmstad, Sweden. Other awards that she stockpiled over her 28-year career include Rolex Player of the Year (1984, 1989 and 1993) as well as the Vare Trophy (1987 and 1993), which is given to the golfer with the lowest scoring average for the season.

After accepting Christ and subsequently getting more involved with the LPGA Fellowship, King made a natural progression toward community outreach and ministry. Although she participated in service projects while part of a high-school group called the Brotherhood Club, the concept of orchestrated serving was relatively new.

"Through the fellowship, we had some opportunities to serve," King says. "We did several Habitat for Humanity projects. We started by going to the mountains of Tennessee and working on houses there. Chris Stevens—who leads the Fellowship on the LPGA Tour—is from Knoxville, and this area was about an hour from Knoxville. We also spearheaded a project in Arizona one winter, in Guadalupe; and we raised the funds to build a house. We worked on the house for two weeks, and during that time, we probably had 80 players that came, between caddies and players and LPGA staff."

King also worked with Stevens and Drive for Life, which helped raise funds for a village in Tanzania. She traveled to Romania in 1993 and 1994 to visit orphanages and assist an adoption agency seeking to place children with American families. King has also traveled to Korea and Japan, where she shared her testimony with various golf groups, and she has consistently participated in FCA golf camps as well.

In January 2005, King went to Honduras with LPGA golfer Hilary Lunke (and her husband, Tyler) to help build houses with World Vision, a humanitarian organization for which she has the utmost respect and admiration. Her association with the group has also helped her identify a greater understanding of serving.

"Serving is helping others without any expectations in return," King says. "I think about Mother Teresa. She helped people without any expectations. World Vision is a Christian organization, but it's not like every time they go to serve someone, there's an expectation that they have to share their faith. They work in some countries where it's illegal to share your faith, but they are serving in the name of Christ because Christ called us to serve. If those opportunities arise, if someone asks, 'Why are you doing this?' then they can say, 'It's because of my love of Christ.'"

King also points to the example of Christ Himself, who first served the people's physical needs before speaking to their spiritual needs, with no prerequisites or demands to be met first.

"You can't go to someone who is starving to death and not help them physically and still expect them to want to listen to a message of Christ," claims King. "That's like saying, 'God loves you and I love you, but I'm not willing to help you.'"

As she continued to learn about serving, it became clear that her competitive golf career was nearing its end. In June 2005, her father was diagnosed with terminal cancer. Just three months later, he passed away. King was then faced with the challenge of caring for her mother who suffered with Alzheimer's disease until she passed away in April 2007. In addition to handling these family crises, King was dealing with personal wear and tear, the natural result of nearly 30 years on the LPGA Tour. She retired in 2005, and shoulder surgery in 2006 effectively sealed the deal.

But that same year, King discovered new life within the golfing world when she was selected to be the 2007 U.S. team captain at the prestigious Solheim Cup—the women's equivalent of the Ryder Cup. She was a natural fit for the head-to-head competition, having previously played in the event five times herself. And this time, it was going to be about much more than the game of golf.

"I decided I wanted to use that platform to do something," King reveals. "I read a book called *The End of Poverty: Economic Possibilities of Our Time* by Jeffrey Sachs. So I called Dana Buck, my contact at World Vision, and told him I wanted to do something, and I felt like I was being led to do something in Africa. He told me I needed to go over there, and they were putting together a group of women to go over there. So I ended up going there in 2006."

After an exploratory trip that took King to Tanzania, Kenya, Rwanda and Zambia, she returned with the inspiration for a nonprofit organization appropriately named Golf Fore Africa. The organization's purpose is "to raise funds and awareness within the golf community to help those who have been infected or are affected by AIDS." The LPGA lent its support to King's first project in Rwanda, and to date close to $200,000 in donations have been collected.

"So basically, we exist to be a fund-raising body to help people who are already on the ground doing the work," King says. "We'll go over there to make sure that what we've raised is being used effectively. But the most effective thing to do is to give your money to help those that are there that have the expertise. That's a part of service."

"I'm being an advocate," she continues. "I can speak out. I've gone and seen it firsthand, and I think that's why they want us to go. That's what God calls us to do. It's like when Jesus healed the paralytic who wanted to stick around with Him, He said, 'No, go home, and tell your family what God's done for you and how He's had mercy on you.' That's what I feel I'm called to do too—to talk about what I've seen and to be an advocate for those people."

For King, it's become quite personal. Because of her experiences in Africa, it's more to her than just helping strangers in a strange land. King has met with men, women and children impacted by disease, poverty and war. Those one-on-one human connections have fueled her passion to serve the ones that Jesus referred to in Matthew 25:40 as "the least of these."

"We helped one woman who was 24 years old and was blind," King shares. "She was the head of her household, and she had five siblings. World Vision was providing seeds so that she could plant Irish potatoes in her little plot of land. So we basically did that. We had all of the villagers watching us and laughing at us and then some of the women jumped in and helped us with the hoeing, and they had the babies strapped on their backs. But in that situation, it's more about good will. There's a language barrier, and yet you're showing them that you care. I think that brings dignity to people. What we heard when we met with people was that we came all that way to see them and that showed we cared about them."

King has learned that serving can show the love of Jesus to others without the use of one single word. She has also discovered that taking others along for the ride can have a similar impact and open the door for evangelism. Not all of the people King has brought to Africa have been believers, and some who believe have a level of faith that is evident but not fully developed. In both instances, King has been amazed at how powerful the nature of serving others opens the hearts of those tag-along servants.

"When you have people like professional golfers who make these trips, they're getting a lot of their needs met,"

King says. "You're bringing them into a cause that's bigger than them. That often gives you an opportunity to share your faith. It changes their heart. It's a common ground where you can come together. The people that went with us to Africa, most of them weren't believers. So you're putting them in a situation where they get to see Christians who are different, and they're helping people, and that just might be the introduction that takes them a step along the way."

Not only does King hope to put a dent in many of Africa's problems, but she would also love to see the next generation of servants rise up and get involved with similar worthy and life-changing causes. "When you see what other people are going through," she says, "it tends to put your life in perspective."

For instance, in Rwanda, King saw the tragic results of poverty and AIDS set against a hideous backdrop of war and genocide. She met one Rwandan employed by World Vision who had lost 70 members of her family to the genocide. Amazingly, this woman had courageously moved forward to accept a position titled Head of Healing, Peace and Reconciliation.

"People who come to Rwanda think they have a lot of problems," King says. "But when they see what the people there have to forgive, it makes their problems seem small. I mean they have to forgive the people that have killed their families and their friends that are now coming back into society, and they're living next to them. That's what they're facing now. There are so many things that you learn through serving."

King has also seen the positive impact that the United States government has facilitated through a $30 billion pledge made by President George W. Bush in 2003. She was pleased to hear the president commit an additional $30 billion for AIDS during the 2008 State of the Union address. Because of King's captaincy with the winning Solheim Cup team, she actually had the chance to thank President Bush in person.

As pleased as she was to see that kind of compassion coming from the White House, King has been even more gratified by her opportunity to work alongside and generate support for the unsung heroes of this battle against social injustice.

"I am so inspired by the faith of the Christians who are there every day in the midst of the poverty, trying to make a difference," King says. "I think you're just inspired by those you're serving or those you're serving with—inspired by the beauty of the people. You definitely get a lot more back than what you give. As believers, we're all called to serve. We're all called to witness, to share our story. We're also called to be a part of the community of believers. But He also calls us to a life of service. So really, if you want to be obedient, you need to be serving."

TRAINING TIME

1. Betsy King talks about the need for security versus the struggle for significance. How important is security (financial, relational, spiritual) to you? How often do you find yourself thinking about being a person of significance?

2. Why should you expect nothing in return when serving others? What are some ways that Jesus demonstrated this philosophy throughout His ministry of healing and teaching?

3. Read Matthew 25:31-46. What imagery comes to mind when you hear the phrase "the least of these"? What does the extremity between Jesus' two responses tell you about God's emphasis on serving those in need?

4. Read John 13:35. How do Jesus' words in this passage contrast with what many non-believers think of today's church body? Why is it important for us to show love to one another as well as to those outside of the church walls?

5. What are some ways that serving can change the heart of the servant? How can serving open the hearts of those being served? Can you describe a time when you've seen one or both of these scenarios played out in your own acts of service?

"In 2005, I went to Tanzania on a photography safari with some friends. Three of us were turning 50. All of us were believers. We weren't really around the poverty except one day when we went to a fishing village on Lake Victoria that was very poor. We flew in and out of an airport at Kilimanjaro, and then a year later I was back at that same airport. I thought, *This is a place I'd never thought I'd be again*. I went with a friend, and we went to Tanzania first because her cousin was living there and building a school for AIDS orphans. Then we met up with a group in Kenya and also went to Rwanda and Zambia with World Vision. I didn't know much about AIDS, and it was just eye-opening for me to see the devastation in Africa caused by poverty and AIDS and other illnesses. People here in the United State don't have a clue. We talk about the poor in America, but generally the poor here have some sort of safety net. Over there, you have 70 or 80 percent of the people living below the poverty line, and there isn't any social safety net from the government. It's just an entirely different situation. In Rwanda, 20 percent of the kids die by age five. There's a 50 percent unemployment rate. I mean, people go nuts over here when it's 5 percent. It's a totally different picture."

—Betsy King

SHARED TALENTS

Mike Minter
Former NFL Safety

In every way I've shown you that by laboring like this, it is necessary
to help the weak and to keep in mind the words of the Lord Jesus,
for He said, "It is more blessed to give than to receive."

ACTS 20:35

There is no greater calling than to serve your fellow men.
There is no greater contribution than to help the weak. There is no
greater satisfaction than to have done it well.

WALTER REUTHER

Taking life for granted and daydreaming about greener pastures are things everyone does at one time or another. They are so common, in fact, that they've been the centerpieces of countless offerings from the entertainment world over the past 60 years. Feature films ranging from 1946's *It's A Wonderful Life* (starring Jimmy Stewart) to 1988's *Big* (starring Tom Hanks) and 1990's *Mr. Destiny* (starring Jim Belushi) have all tackled the subject.

Not to be left out, the music industry has a history of addressing the topic in such hit songs, among others, as Joni Mitchell's 1970 folk tune "Big Yellow Taxi" and the more overtly stated 1988 rock ballad "Don't Know What You Got (Till It's Gone)," performed by old-school metal icons Cinderella.

Most of the time, people who fall prey to this syndrome aren't visited by an angel to show them what life would be like without them. They usually don't travel to an alternate reality where everything they dreamed about comes true, only to realize how much they miss their former existence. It's not always as blatant as the strike of a lightning bolt, a mysterious message from a stranger or the writing on the wall. But the reality that life is bigger than one individual eventually makes itself known.

Just ask former Carolina Panthers' star defensive back Mike Minter. His life-altering moment came in 1994 as a sophomore at Nebraska. Just two games into the season, Minter found himself in uncharted territory. He was lying on the field, writhing in pain, having just torn the anterior cruciate ligament (ACL) in his left knee. Unsure of what this injury meant to his football future, Minter was profoundly impacted by the unfortunate circumstance.

"When football was taken away, it was like, *What am I doing? What is life all about?*" he recalls. "I thought football was all there was. I was laying there on the ground looking up, and I didn't have football anymore. I didn't know what to do."

It was in that moment of forced introspection when Minter's self-centered mindset started to slowly shift toward a greater understanding of serving. Strangely, though, he had seen plenty of examples of selfless behavior most of his life. He can laugh now at the realization that it took him 20 years to understand the concept, and Minter's present-day understanding makes him appreciate those who quietly laid that foundation.

"My first example of serving was probably through my grandmother," Minter says. "We were kind of at our grandmother's house at a young age, until she passed away when I was seven years old. She would give of herself to her kids and to her grandkids. That was where it all started. And then my mom was just like that. When people needed something, they always came to my mom, and she would always be the one that provided shelter for people. We didn't have much, but she would provide food for others."

Born in Cleveland, Ohio, Minter's family moved to Lawton, Oklahoma, when he was just eight months old, where they lived with his grandmother. He spent the rest of his childhood there and eventually graduated from Lawton High School, where he excelled in both football and basketball. After graduating in 1992, he accepted a scholarship from the University of Nebraska and went to play for legendary head coach Tom Osborne.

Minter didn't see his first action on the field until 1993 as a redshirt freshman. During that season he played as a backup safety, but he showed signs of future greatness with 21 tackles, 2 forced fumbles and 1 sack. It was during his sophomore year that the ACL injury occurred in the second game, forcing him to watch from the sidelines as his Cornhuskers won the national championship.

As a junior, Minter came back impressively to reclaim his starting position, and in the process he helped lead Nebraska to a successful title defense. This was the Cornhuskers' first claim to two consecutive back-to-back national championships in 40 years. Minter then wrapped up his collegiate career by earning All-Big 12 First Team honors with 51 tackles, 5 interceptions and 6 pass deflections.

But more importantly, the future NFL star began to grow in his faith, thanks to an unlikely duo—a baby boy and a coaching legend. "My wife [Kim] and I had our first son [Michael] and I began to think about life and how I was going to teach him about life," Minter says. "Then there was Coach Osborne, who was very consistent—a man who was very stable. I used to wonder how and why, and I wanted to be like him. All of these things were making me question what life was all about."

Minter didn't stop there. He took his desire for knowledge and put it into action. Minter took full advantage of Nebraska's historically strong FCA program, where Coach Osborne was (and still is) not only a strong supporter but also an active participant in that organization. Through that mentoring process, Minter—who describes himself as "a thinker"—began searching to find the meaning of life from a biblical perspective.

"Even though I wasn't saved, I always knew there was a God, and I just didn't know how to get to Him," Minter says. "I just started researching different religions, and somebody told me about Jesus Christ and who He was and what He did for us and how He came to Earth to die for us, and this is how we get to heaven—and you don't have to do anything. All you have to do is accept what He has done. You don't have to go lift weights and be the fastest kid on the field. All you have to do is sign up. And I said, 'Man, that's the greatest gift of all. He's going to take all of these things I've done in my life and forgive them and give me joy. That's where it's at.'"

That decision compelled Minter to get on his knees and pray for God's forgiveness as well as a greater desire to know his Creator. He knew that God had the answers to all of his many questions and was ready to start the learning process. Minter says one thing he began understanding right away was the biblical principle of serving, and it was when he accepted Christ that he recognized a previously hidden talent.

"My calling is to show people the potential they have inside of them and how God sees them," Minter says. "God has given me a blessing to be able to look at people and see their potential. I look at anybody, and God will show me their potential. That's what I cling to."

One of Minter's earliest opportunities to exercise his gifting came at the Orange Bowl, where he was able to visit a project in Miami. He was amazed to discover just how much impact a simple message of hope such as his could have on others.

"The first thing that I saw was kids who didn't really know how much they're loved by God," Minter says. "They didn't know how much they had. All of the sudden, I got to talking to them about Jesus and about how much He loves them and how much He wants them to be what He has called them to be. Then all of the sudden, I started to see the lights come on. There isn't anything like that."

Minter's ability to affect lives in a positive manner greatly increased in 1997 when he was selected by the Carolina Panthers in the second round of the NFL Draft. By the sixth game of the season, the rookie defensive back had earned a starting spot that—outside of 10 games missed in 1998 due to staph infection and two games in 2001 due to an injury—he would not relinquish until his retirement nine years later.

In 2003, Minter anchored the defense that led Carolina to an American Football Conference championship and the franchise's first Super Bowl appearance. The Panthers lost a hard-fought game against the New England Patriots, 32-29, but Minter made his presence felt with a career high 18 tackles. Even more amazing than Minter's individual effort was the fact that he played most of the second half on a broken left foot but did not reveal his injury until after the game.

Off the field, Minter was seeking out ways to serve others. His home church in Charlotte had built a day-care center, and the idea inspired him to do something similar for the surrounding community. But Minter wasn't interested in a solo venture. Instead, he was looking for solid partnerships that would stand the test of time.

"God laid on my heart to get NFL guys together in business," Minter says. "In the NFL, what happens is you have a player maybe over here doing something and a player over there doing something, but they never come together. You never have that power together. So God laid on my heart to bring NFL guys together and use what we have learned and seen over the years."

Minter looked no further than his own team for support. He joined forces with defensive end Mike Rucker, wide receiver Muhsin Muhammad and running back Steven Davis. Although Muhammad and Davis eventually left Carolina (Muhammad played for Chicago before returning to Carolina in 2008, while Davis moved on to St. Louis before retiring after the 2006 season), the four-man partnership has remained intact throughout the process.

The end result was Ruckus House—a day-care and learning center that focuses on shaping the lives of children through education and Christian values. Minter and his team opened the first facility in Harrisburg, North Carolina, during the spring of 2005.

"When you bring education, kids, faith and football all together, you will have a dynamic combination," Minter says. "They [Rucker, Muhammad and Davis] all have kids, and they agreed. They all understood the importance of education at an early age, and all of them are saved and understood the importance of having faith and instilling the characteristics of God into kids early on. So that's how the Ruckus House came about. That's how it happened."

On August 7, 2007, Minter officially retired as an NFL athlete. In nine seasons with Carolina, he set team records for game starts (141), consecutive starts (94), fumble recoveries (8) and interceptions for touchdowns (4). Minter also ended his career with 790 tackles and 15 interceptions, making him one of the franchise's most prolific defensive players.

As difficult as it was for Minter to walk away from the game he loves, he is thankful that even greater opportunities were already awaiting him outside of the stadium. That future included the launch of a second Ruckus House in Concord, North Carolina, and plans to expand the program across the state and perhaps nationally as well.

"It's been unbelievable to see everything that's been going on," Minter says. "Kids are changing. Parents are changing. As a matter of fact, I just heard a story about how a kid changed and was praying after hearing a Christian song. The mom just pulled off to the side of the road and started crying, because she was so touched by this. That was something that blew my mind. We're doing what God called us to do."

Minter's heart for serving goes well beyond his involvement with Ruckus House. In March 2007, he visited the African nations of Senegal and Gambia. While there, he visited facilities that had been set up by the YMCA. (Minter is a member of the board of directors of the YMCA of Greater Charlotte.)

"I've always wanted to go to Africa," Minter reveals. "That was a big thing for me. What it showed me was how connected all of us are. We're so connected. In America, we have a tendency to just think about America. It opened my eyes to the world and how connected we are. If one thing gets affected by something, it affects everybody else."

Minter says there are far too many stories from his trip to be recounted in a short period of time. One of the most memorable moments, however, came when he made his first visit to an orphanage.

"I've never been called to adopt, so I just didn't un-derstand that," Minter says. "My wife always said she wanted to adopt when our kids get older, and I've been like, 'I don't know about that.' So we went to the orphan-age; there were about 25 babies there, and I thought I was just going to hold one of them and play with them and then leave. But all of the sudden, my heart just connected to these babies. These babies reminded me of myself. It began to show me how important and how great it is for people to give of their own love and life and home to be able to help kids and babies that don't have that oppor-tunity. And it just blew my mind. It softened my heart on adoption and how important it is."

Since that life-altering moment in 1994 as a confused, injured young athlete, Minter has continued to learn about and embrace the value of serving as modeled by Jesus. He can see a marked difference in the people-centered man he is today as opposed to the self-centered man he was just a few years ago. Minter also has a greater understanding of the purpose behind blessings and success, which can be found in the parable of the talents.

Found in Matthew 25:14-30, Jesus tells a story of a master who travels away from home for an extended period of time but first leaves three of his servants with the responsibility of taking care of his money. He leaves each servant a different amount of money. The first two take their money (or talents) and multiply it through various business dealings and ventures. The third servant is afraid of losing his money, so he buries it until the master returns. On his return, the master praises the first two servants and gives them even greater responsibility, but he scolds the third servant and throws him out of his house.

"God blessed these people with these different talents, and they had to do something with it," Minter explains. "One buried his and didn't do anything with it, and God came back and said, 'Wicked man. You didn't do what you were supposed to do.' One multiplied his talent a little bit and the other maximized his to the fullest. That's where I feel like I sit. And it wasn't theirs to keep. It was to give to other people."

Minter has also learned the truth found in Acts 20:35, in which followers of Jesus are reminded that it is necessary to help the weak and that it is more blessed to give

141

than to receive. "That Scripture right there is so true," he says. "It's absolutely a promise. The more you give, guess what? The more God can say, 'Okay, now let Me give you more.' If you come with your hands closed because you don't want to let go of what you have, then God can no longer put anything in your hands. You've got to open them up and let Him have His will to put and take whatever He wants into and out of your hands. That's how I look at it."

Sometimes Minter finds himself frustrated with other Christians who struggle with serving. He feels that one of the greatest dangers is when people take ownership of the church and use phrases like, "It's my church" or "My church did it." Minter warns that taking a position of ownership leads to a loss of focus.

Minter also believes that too many believers are caught up in their circumstances and don't realize that God can use them to serve no matter where they are in life. Just like the three servants in the Parable of the Talents, we are all given different measures of blessings. It's up to each of us to decide whether we will multiply those gifts or hide them where no one else can be impacted with the gospel of salvation and hope.

"Don't worry about tomorrow," Minter says. "You maximize where you're at today. If you maximize where you're at, you're going to fulfill what God has for you right now. Don't look at what the next man has. That's not what God's called you to do. He's called you to that specific situation for that specific time. We've got to understand that, because we have a tendency to look at other people and what they're doing. But that may not be doing what God wants you to be doing. Maximize where you're at, and God will take you to where you need to be."

TRAINING TIME

1. When Mike Minter tore his ACL as a sophomore at Nebraska, he contemplated his future and his purpose in life. Can you describe a time when life-changing circumstances had you asking similar questions?

2. It took Minter the responsibility of fatherhood and the mentoring influence of Coach Tom Osborne for him to understand the importance of serving. What individuals or life situations have helped you come to the same revelations?

3. Read Matthew 25:14-30. What are the different personality traits displayed in the first two servants as opposed to the third servant? Why do you think the master was so upset at the third servant? What is the message of this parable as it relates to serving?

4. Read Acts 20:35. Think of a time when you received a gift. Now think of a time when you gave someone else a gift. How did each of the scenarios make you feel? Which was more gratifying? Why?

5. Minter says, "Maximize where you're at and God will take you to where you need to be." How might a lack of position or resource stop you from serving? What are some ways that you can serve in spite of such limitations?

"The Holy Spirit's job is to change you, to empower you to change. In that process of giving you the power to change, this is when you begin to know that life is not about you. When you understand that, then you begin to understand about serving. Until you get it out of your mind that life is about you, you can't serve right. That's where it began with me. I read the Bible from front to back, and in that process, I started seeing that life is not about Mike Minter. It's bigger than Mike Minter, and it's about God and His plan. What God gives you is not for you. It's for other people. It's not out of obligation. It's not because you think you're supposed to do it. True serving from the heart is when you understand God has given you things for other people, not for you. It's just like the story in the Bible where Jesus is washing His disciples' feet. He's telling them, 'Guys, this is bigger than you. You can't be so big that you can't wash your brother's feet or let your brother wash your feet.' This is what has to happen. So for me, God is using football for a stepping-stone to take me to the next level, so when I speak, people are going to listen. It's amazing what God uses. He uses a game like football so that we can have a platform to be able to speak for His glory."

—Mike Minter

SUBTLETIES OF SERVING

John Wooden
Former UCLA Head Men's Basketball Coach

Now these three remain: faith, hope, and love.
But the greatest of these is love.

1 CORINTHIANS 13:13

We all have the means to bestow on others the most lavish gifts:
love, joy, peace, hope, kindness, acceptance, encouragement,
laughter, forgiveness, time. There is not enough money to
buy them and not too little money to give them.

EDEN ELIOT

When you are a sports legend like Coach John Wooden, the opportunity to give of your time and resources can be found waiting around every corner. People have been looking to attach his name to charitable causes and have been chasing him down for personal appearances ever since he became synonymous with college basketball greatness.

Wooden, being the servant leader that he is, has graciously accepted many offers over the years. He has visited numerous veterans' hospitals and children's hospitals.

In fact, it's organizations that support kids that really get his attention.

"I've always had a particular love and empathy for children," Wooden says. "I have cherished times when I have been able to hold a newborn in my arms. I especially remember holding astronaut Sally Ride and [former] Stanford basketball coach Mike Montgomery when they were babies. I was pleased when the organizers of the Wooden Classic Basketball Tournament decided to give a portion of their proceeds to children's hospitals. Now they have money going to the Special Olympics, and that pleases me, too. Needs of children have a special appeal to me. Showing love for these children through these gifts makes me very happy. I know the money doesn't make all of their problems disappear, but it certainly helps make their lives better."

But for Wooden, the act of serving is much more than supporting charities or visiting the sick. In fact, he believes that there are many small, sometimes unnoticeable things that ultimately have a long-lasting impact on others.

"There is always great joy in learning that something you've said or done has been meaningful to another," Wooden says. "Especially when you do it without any thought of receiving anything in return. Your gift doesn't even have to be material. Helping others in any way—with a smile, a nod or a pat on the back—warms the heart."

Wooden transferred that philosophy to his style of coaching. He always strived to help his players understand what it looked like to serve others both on and off the court. "If a player scored off a pass, I wanted him to point to the man giving the assist until they made eye contact in a gesture of thanks and acknowledgement," he says. "I started that with my high school teams. I also wanted a gesture of thanks done for a good pick, for help on defense or for any other good play. Kindness makes for much better teamwork."

Wooden also taught his players how to serve others with acts of kindness and consideration. Even when his teams at UCLA were winning a record 10 NCAA men's basketball National Championships (including another record-setting 7 consecutive titles), he still required his players to think of others first—a rarity in a sports world of today that is often dominated by self-serving high-profile athletes.

"I don't believe a year ever went by when I didn't receive a letter from a custodian from one of the arenas where we played, indicating that we left the dressing room cleaner than anybody else," Wooden recalls. "I wouldn't allow [the team] to leave until the orange peels, gum wrappers, towels and soap chips were off the floor."

One of the first subtle acts of serving that Wooden learned was from his father, Joshua Wooden. He instilled many great qualities in his four sons, but it was the spiritual fruit of gentleness that left an indelible mark on Coach Wooden. This is something that he has since learned to appreciate even more through the teaching found in 2 Timothy 2:24-25, which states, "The Lord's slave must not quarrel, but must be gentle to everyone, able to teach, and patient, instructing his opponents with gentleness. Perhaps God will grant them repentance to know the truth."

"My dad influenced me in many ways," Wooden says. "He was physically strong, but he wasn't a huge man. Because he knew how to use his leverage, he could lift and move things around that stronger people could not. He was powerful, but he was also kind and gentle. I never heard him say an unkind word about anyone, nor did I ever hear him utter a word of profanity. I saw my dad's gentle spirit on display when he worked with fractious horses and with dogs I thought were vicious. There's nothing stronger than gentleness. My dad was the epitome of this principle."

149

Wooden displayed that same gentleness when dealing with his players. Even when correcting his players, he found ways to do so without demeaning or berating them. "Some of my players needed a pat on the back," Wooden says. "For others, the pat needed to be a little lower and a little firmer."

That was Wooden's way. He never shied away from discipline, but he always doled it out in a way that allowed them to "know the truth." It's that unique approach that has caused many to refer to Wooden not only as the greatest coach of our time but also as the greatest teacher to grace college athletics—a teacher who daily used the court as his classroom.

Wooden himself says he considers himself to be more of a teacher than a coach. Take, for instance, the times he stood up for racial equality while he was a high school coach in Indiana and head coach at Indiana State. Some may have taken his actions as a way for him to make a socio-political statement, but for Wooden, he was teaching his players and the supporting communities about integrity and respect. "The most important profession in the world is parenting," Wooden says. "The second is teaching, and everyone is a teacher to someone."

Coach Wooden has also been a devoted friend to many players, assistant coaches and athletic administrators over the years. The act of friendship is yet another one of those subtleties of serving that has had a significant impact on other people's lives. Wooden's basis for this belief can be found in Ecclesiastes 4:12, which says, "If somebody overpowers one person, two can resist him. A cord of three strands is not easily broken."

"God created us to be interdependent," Wooden says. "We were not designed to go through life alone. We become so much more when we come alongside others—and we make them better, too. . . . Friends help complete us, and we'll be better for having taken them along on our journey to becoming all we are capable of becoming."

Yet none of these subtle aspects of serving—sharing, consideration, gentleness, teaching or friendship—will matter much without the most powerful force known to mankind: love. One of Wooden's favorite passages,

1 Corinthians 13 (commonly referred to as the "love chapter"), warns that all of the acts of kindness, giving, faith or even prophecy will have no value to God if love is not at the root of one's motivation.

"Love is the greatest word in our language," Wooden says. "When we have love, many of our problems disappear. Differences are manageable when love has its way. I'm sure my regard for love comes from my reading of the Bible. . . . We can give without loving, but we can't love without giving. In fact, love is nothing unless we give it to someone."

TRAINING TIME

1. John Wooden says, "Helping others in any way—with a smile, a nod or a pat—warms the heart." Can you recall a time when someone's simple act of service brightened your day?

2. Wooden talks about how he required his players to be thoughtful by picking up the locker room after road games. How does that match up with the mentality of today's stereotypical college or pro athlete? How can being considerate of others equate to the act of serving?

3. Read 2 Timothy 2:24-25. What does this passage tell you about the role gentleness plays in the life of a servant? What are some ways that you can exhibit this trait to those around you?

4. Read Ecclesiastes 4:12. Can you describe a situation in which a good friend helped you weather a personal storm? How has your friendship helped that person deal with the inevitable trials of his or her life? In what ways can you serve your friends?

5. Read 1 Corinthians 13:1-3. Why do you think love is such a key component in authentic serving? What do you think Wooden meant when he said that "love is nothing unless we give it to someone"? What are some ways that you can give love to someone else?

"After I graduated from Purdue University, I coached high school basketball in Indiana. One day, we were headed to Cincinnati for a game. However, the mother of one of the players did not want her son to go along, because he would be competing against an African-American player on the opposing squad. This was before Martin Luther King Jr.'s speech, the March on Washington or any of the Civil Rights breakthroughs of the 1960s. But I instinctively knew what was right. Dad had helped set my thinking in place on the issue of race. Many times he told my brothers and me, 'Don't consider yourself superior to anyone else, but never feel inferior.' I told the player's mother that if her son didn't play in Cincinnati, he wouldn't play in any other games, either. She relented, and he got in the game. When I coached at Indiana State University in 1946, we had a reserve who was black. When we won our league, we were invited to compete in the NAIA tournament in Kansas City, but tournament officials would not allow us to bring him. Again, I knew what was right, so we didn't go. In these instances, I wasn't really trying to make a political statement; I just wanted to do what was right. . . . One of my players once gave me a great compliment. He said, 'Coach Wooden doesn't see race. He's just looking for players who will play together.' Hearing that gave me about as good a feeling as I could ever have."

—John Wooden

THANKS

Fellowship of Christian Athletes would like to give honor and glory to our Lord and Savior Jesus Christ for the opportunities we have been given to impact so many lives and for everyone who has come alongside us in this ministry.

The four core values are at the heart of what we do and teach. Many people have helped make this series of books on these values a reality. We extend a huge thanks to Chad Bonham for his many hours of hard work in interviewing, writing, compiling and editing. These books would not have been possible without him. Thanks also to Chad's wife, Amy, and his two young sons, Lance and Cole (who was born just about the time the manuscript went to the publisher).

We also want to thank the following people and groups for their vital contributions: Les Steckel, John Wooden, Tony Dungy, Jackie Cook, the Indianapolis Colts, Shaun Alexander, Todd Gowin, Lane Gammel, the Seattle Seahawks, Mike Minter, Teddi Domann, Kayla Ravenkamp, Domann & Pittman Football, Danny Wuerffel, Beverly Tillery, Desire Street Ministries, Pat Williams, Andrew Herdliska, the Orlando Magic, Jarome Iginla, Peter Hanlon, the Calgary Flames, Tim Tebow, Zack Higbee, John Hines, University of Florida Media Relations, Betsy King, Ruth Riley, Leigh Anne Gullett, the San Antonio Silver Stars, Michael Chang, Caroline Wong-Nakata, Chang

Family Foundation, Drew Dyck, *New Man Magazine* and Dave Bartlett.

Thanks to the entire FCA staff, who every day faithfully serve coaches and athletes. Thanks to our CEO and president, Les Steckel, for believing in this project. Thanks to the Home Office staff: Bethany Hermes, Tom Rogeberg, Jill Ewert, Shea Vailes and Ken Williams. Thanks also to Bill Greig III, Bill Schultz, Steven Lawson, Mark Weising, Aly Hawkins and everyone at Regal Books.

Impacting the World for Christ Through Sports

FELLOWSHIP OF CHRISTIAN ATHLETES

Since 1954, the Fellowship of Christian Athletes has challenged athletes and coaches to impact the world for Jesus Christ. FCA is cultivating Christian principles in local communities nationwide by encouraging, equipping, and empowering others to serve as examples and make a difference. Reaching more than 2 million people annually on the professional, college, high school, junior high and youth levels, FCA has grown into the largest sports ministry in the world. Through FCA's Four Cs of Ministry—coaches, campus, camps, and community—and the shared passion for athletics and faith, lives are changed for current and future generations.

Fellowship of Christian Athletes
8701 Leeds Road • Kansas City, MO 64129
www. fca.org • fca@fca.org • 1-800-289-0909

COMPETITORS FOR CHRIST

Fellowship of Christian Athletes
Competitor's Creed

I am a Christian first and last.
I am created in the likeness of God Almighty to bring Him glory.
I am a member of Team Jesus Christ.
I wear the colors of the cross.

I am a Competitor now and forever.
I am made to strive, to strain, to stretch and to succeed in the arena of competition.
I am a Christian Competitor and as such, I face my challenger with the face of Christ.

I do not trust in myself.
I do not boast in my abilities or believe in my own strength.
I rely solely on the power of God.
I compete for the pleasure of my Heavenly Father, the honor
of Christ and the reputation of the Holy Spirit.

My attitude on and off the field is above reproach—my conduct beyond criticism.
Whether I am preparing, practicing or playing,
I submit to God's authority and those He has put over me.
I respect my coaches, officials, teammates, and competitors out of respect for the Lord.

My body is the temple of Jesus Christ.
I protect it from within and without.
Nothing enters my body that does not honor the Living God.
My sweat is an offering to my Master. My soreness is a sacrifice to my Savior.

I give my all—all the time.
I do not give up. I do not give in. I do not give out.
I am the Lord's warrior—a competitor by conviction and a disciple of determination.
I am confident beyond reason because my confidence lies in Christ.
The results of my effort must result in His glory.

Let the competition begin.
Let the glory be God's.

Sign the Creed • Go to www.fca.org

FELLOWSHIP OF CHRISTIAN ATHLETES
COACH'S MANDATE

Pray as though nothing of eternal value is going
to happen in my athletes' lives unless God does it.

Prepare each practice and game as giving "my utmost for His highest."

Seek not to be served by my athletes for personal gain, but seek
to serve them as Christ served the church.

Be satisfied not with producing a good record, but with producing good athletes.

Attend carefully to my private and public walk with God, knowing that the
athlete will never rise to a standard higher than that being lived by the coach.

Exalt Christ in my coaching, trusting the Lord will then draw athletes to Himself.

Desire to have a growing hunger for God's Word, for personal
obedience, for fruit of the spirit and for saltiness in competition.

Depend solely upon God for transformation—one athlete at a time.

Preach Christ's word in a Christ-like demeanor, on and off the field of competition.

Recognize that it is impossible to bring glory to both myself
and Christ at the same time.

Allow my coaching to exude the fruit of the Spirit,
thus producing Christ-like athletes.

Trust God to produce in my athletes His chosen purposes,
regardless of whether the wins are readily visible.

Coach with humble gratitude, as one privileged to be God's coach.

FELLOWSHIP OF
CHRISTIAN ATHLETES